ISLAND
OF SECRETS

*The Discovery and
Exploration of Easter Island*

by
JACEK MACHOWSKI

Translated by
Maurice Michael

ROBERT HALE · LONDON

ISBN 0 7091 4870 4

Robert Hale & Company
Clerkenwell House
Clerkenwell Green
London EC1R 0HT

Composed by Specialised Offset Services Ltd.
and printed in Great Britain by
Redwood Burn Limited, Trowbridge & Esher

CONTENTS

1 Easter Island   9
2 The Dutch Discoverers   17
3 The Conquistadors in the Pacific   29
4 English Seamen and the Mysterious Isle   41
5 French Gentlemen and Polynesian Beauties   49
6 Russian Explorers   57
7 The English Return   65
8 The End of its Greatness   73
9 Hotumatua   83
10 Enter Brother Eyraud   89
11 Bishop Jaussen and the Wood that Talks   109
12 The Visit of the *Hyena*   117
13 An American Expedition   125
14 An English Expedition   145
15 A Franco-Belgian Expedition   157
16 The Descendants of Maklaj   169
17 The Viking of the Pacific   175
18 The Three Theories   193
Conclusion   203
Chronology of Events   205
List of the Legendary Kings   209
Bibliography   211
Index   217

ILLUSTRATIONS

Easter Islanders on the deck of a European ship   32
Easter Island women and European sailors on the shore, drawings made by members of the early expeditions   32
Sketches of the statues made by members of the nineteenth-century expeditions   33
Stone statues on the slopes of the volcano Rano Raraku   48
Easter Island women drawn by Hodges of the Cook expedition   49
Estevan, drawn by Miklucho-Maklaj   49
Man and woman of Easter Island, drawn by Radiguet   49
Statue with its head-covering of volcanic tufa   80
An unfinished statue in the crater quarry on Rano Raraku   81
Hopu, having found the egg of the *manu-tara*, presents it to his *matato*   81
Rock drawings and bas reliefs of *tangata-manu*   96
Various drawings of the man-bird, *tangata-manu*   97
Drawings on the inner walls of the stone dwellings of Orongo   112
Entrance to the stone dwellings of Orongo   112
Small wooden and stone carvings made by Easter Island artists   113
One of the mysterious carved hands brought from Easter Island   113
Two examples of *kohau rongo-rongo*   128
Fragment of Tomeniki's book   128
Reconstructing the Akiwi *ahu* using the islanders' traditional method   129
Raising statues using modern means   129

LINE FIGURES IN THE TEXT

Page

Map of Easter Island made by the Spanish expedition
of 1770   35
'Signatures' of the leaders of Easter Island appended
to the 'treaty' with Spain, 1770   38
Stone tomb at the foot of Rano Raraku, as drawn by
Weisser   120
Bas relief of a deity discovered by Geiseler on the inner
wall to one of the stone dwellings of Orongo   122
Section and perspective of the *ahu* platform according
to Scoresby-Routledge   155
Fragments of the notes of the Descendents of Maklaj.
Comparison of hieroglyphs from the Indus valley and
Easter Island, made by David Diringer   171
Part of the headman's book brought back from Easter
Island by the Heyerdahl Expedition   191

MAP   10

I

EASTER ISLAND

Easter Island is the loneliest and most isolated spot on our planet. Surrounded by the limitless waters of the Pacific it is nearly a thousand miles from land. For centuries the nearest fixed points on which its inhabitants could fix their gaze were the stars and the moon. Yet this tiny island set in the immensity of the largest of our oceans has provided anthropologists, archaeologists, philologists and historians of art with sensational material and set them puzzles that they have still not solved. From the time of its discovery nearly two and a half centuries ago a nimbus of mystery has surrounded Easter Island. Being itself such a puzzle, it has drawn the attention of many scientists hoping perhaps to find there the key to other problems.

Easter Island is of volcanic origin. It rises to some 1900 feet above sea level and covers an area of 118 square kilometres. Interest in it was aroused quite early, but for long years it remained as inaccessible to scientists and their research as the moon, so that they had only secondhand information to go on. The early visitors to the island were not all gifted with scientific accuracy. Many had lively imaginations and a tendency to exaggerate. Though most of the early voyages of discovery included a scientist (Behrens, Forster, Chamisso) among the members of the expedition, the shortness of their stay, sometimes just a few hours, did not permit of exact scientific description of the main features of the island and its inhabitants.

It was only at the turn of the twentieth century that scientists began investigating the island, at first rather haphazardly, then more systematically. The first proper scientific expedition demonstrated that it had come a century at least too late. Internecine strife among the islanders, battles with white intruders and raiding slave-traders, the barbaric methods of missionaries had wrought irreparable damage. The magnificent memorials of the islanders' ancient culture

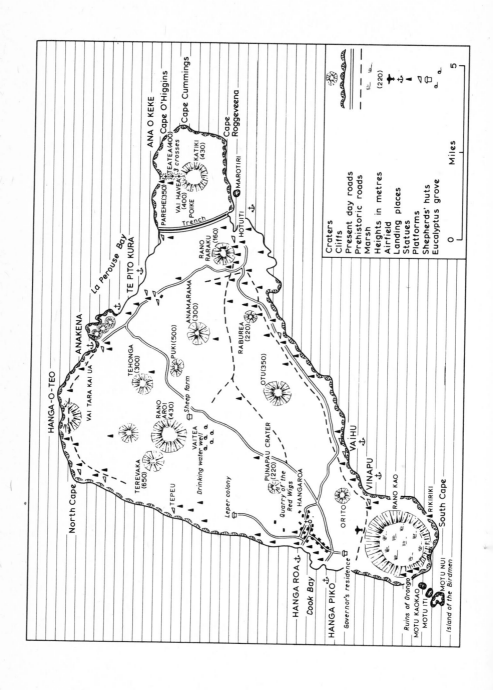

had been reduced to a state of complete ruin, while that mysterious race, the Easter Islanders themselves, had been wellnigh exterminated, so that their culture had been destroyed and with it the island's individuality.

The use of scientific methods has considerably extended the horizons of our knowledge of the island, its people and their culture. Many a legend, hypothesis and falsification has been destroyed by its uncompromising blows, yet the island has never lost its reputation and attraction as an island of mystery. Indeed, many of the island's puzzles are still not solved 250 years after its discovery. Only time will show whether they ever can be. The aim of this book is to present a chronological account of the efforts of explorers, sailors and scientists to solve the island's mysteries, especially the three main ones: the stone statues, the islanders' script and their origins.

THE STONE STATUES

Easter Island is mainly famous for its enormous stone statues. They are and will always be symbols of its mysterious past. The presence of such things on this lonely, poor, little island cut off from the rest of the world by the watery wastes of earth's largest ocean amazed its first European discoverer and today still intrigues academics and laymen alike.

It was an unusual sight that met the eyes of the first ship's company to approach the island: the stony beaches, the extensive grasslands covering the interior and the slopes of the extinct volcanoes were dotted with huge stone statues, many of them the height of a house of several storeys. At first glance they all looked alike, as if mass-produced, yet on examination they proved to differ in size and in a number of details. They ranged in height from three feet to eighty feet, so that the highest were almost as tall as a modern eight-storey building and only insignificantly lower than the famous Colossus of Rhodes (97 feet) accounted one of the seven wonders of the ancient world.

The extensive slopes of the extinct volcano Rano Raraku were peppered with statues of various sizes which the islanders called *moai*. Most were just flat faces; some torsos and heads, the latter having ears prolonged downwards, unusual stone headcoverings cylindrical in shape and made of red lava. Some had arms and hands hanging at their sides or laid flat on their stomachs.

In various part of the island were extensive terraced stone platforms, measuring from as few score feet to several hundred yards in length, some 30 yards in width and 16 feet in height. These the natives called *ahu*. On these *ahu* in the old days there used to stand rows of anything up to fifteen of the huge stone statues all turned with their backs to the sea and thus facing the interior of the island. There were over 500 of these stone giants on this relatively tiny island giving it the semblance of a devastated giant cemetery with its tombs in various states of dilipidation.

The discovery of these statues caused a sensation, expecially as the other islands scattered about the vast expanse of the Pacific between Asia, Australia and South America were inhabited by peoples at a rather low stage of development. There was no doubt that these statues could only be the work of people of a highly developed culture. But who had made them? And why were they made and amassed in such numbers on such a tiny patch of land? Many people have tried to answer these questions, but so far without success.

It was only the actual European discoverers of the island and the crews of the first few ships to follow them who were able to admire these splendid stone statues in all their magnificance on their platforms, for by 1815, when the Russian Kotzebue expedition reached the island, they found most of the statues lying on the ground face down. They had been overthrown during civil strife that had broken out among the islanders at the turn of the century.

The giant statues of Easter Island are just as impressive in their way as are the pyramids of the Egyptian pharaohs, the ancient temples of India or the great buildings of the Aztecs, Mayas and Incas. However remote from each other spatially they all have certain features in common. They all came into being in order to satisfy an inner need of aesthetic creation at the same time as trying to give outward expression to the might of those on whose orders they were erected. The Egyptian, Hindu and South American structures were the creation of powerful states with vast lands and huge populations, but that cannot be said of the stone statues of Easter Island. The presence of these gigantic statues on a tiny island so far from the world's great cultural centres, where everything else is on such a tiny scale, is indeed astounding.

It has been suggested that the purpose of the statues was to protect the island by scaring would-be invaders away, but in that case why were their fierce countenances not turned outwards to face the sea? There are, of course, a number of other arguments against this theory. But, in that case, what was their purpose? Who had them erected and why?

A whole literature has been devoted to this subject without the questions having as yet received a satisfactory answer.

THE WOOD THAT SPEAKS

As if the giant statues of Easter Island were not sensational enough the first European visitors found there wooden tablets covered with unusual hieroglyphs that raised the question: had the earlier inhabitants of the island known the arts of writing and reading? If they had, it would have been extraordinary indeed, for as in all that vast expanse from Asia to South America only one people, the Maoris, have been able to boast of their own writing, an art that is one of the essential distinctions between the primitive and civilized peoples.

For more than a hundred years now people in many countries have been trying to decipher the mysterious hieroglyphs of Easter Island, yet those who have tried have been mostly amateurs. Scientists have shown a surprising indifference to solving this particular puzzle.

The first person to draw attention to the hieroglyphs was the bishop of Tahiti, Jaussen, in whose diocese the island was included in the sixties of last century. The newly converted islanders sent the bishop as a gift a necklace ingeniously plaited of human hair and suspended from it a wooden tablet covered with rows of tiny incised hieroglyphs. The bishop, who had scientific interests, remembered that one of his missionaries, Brother Eyraud, who worked on Easter Island, had mentioned hieroglyphs in one of his reports, so the bishop wrote to him asking him to send him further samples. The request came too late, for the zealous missionaries, regarding the tablets as instruments of a pagan cult, had destroyed all they could lay hands on, even using them as firewood in their kitchens. Now, there seemed to be none left.

Two years later, another missionary, Brother Zumbohm, discovered among some rocks the remains of a tablet badly affected by damp and insects. Carefully he wrapped it up and took it back to the mission to try and preserve it. An islander who worked for the missionaries, seeing how interested Brother Zumbohm was in what he had found, brought him the following day a while tablet of *kohau rongo-rongo*, the wood that talks, in a perfect state of preservation. Unable to decipher it, Brother Zumbohm sent for the most intelligent of the islanders, showed them the tablet and asked them to read it. One took hold of the tablet and, the others grouped round him, they began chanting a sort of song, their eyes following the lines of hieroglyphs. After a couple of verses however they suddenly stopped and began arguing about the text. The differences of opinion seemed irreconcilable and Brother Zumbohm gave up the attempt to decipher the hieroglyphs, packed up the tablets and sent them to the bishop in Tahiti.

Ever since people have been trying to decipher the Easter Island hieroglyphs hoping that this might provide clues as to the origin both of the islanders and of the giant statues. Unfortunately only twenty-five tablets have survived: twenty-one of them only being true *kohau rongo-rongo*, the other four being necklace pendants, *rei-miro*, such as Bishop Jaussen was sent and these have only a few lines of text on them. Today these tablets are in museums in Austria, Belgium, Chile, Germany, Great Britain, Russia and the USA.

Although large rewards have been offered for any more tablets found, none have come to light. Unable to find any originals and tempted by the rewards offered, the islanders tried to imitate them, but they did not possess the skill of their ancestors and the fakes were recognized for what they were.

According to the islanders, to be taught the arts of writing and reading the tablets used to be a privilege reserved for minstrels and reciters, who were called *tangata rongo-rongo*. They were recruited from among the island's aristocracy and many of them were related to the royal family. They were taught genealogies, religious hymns and the island's oral traditions. Facts and legends were taught to each new generation in special schools. For the first lessons in cutting the hieroglyphs they used a sharp shark's tooth on a banana leaf or stalk. Wood was too precious to be used for practice. These pupils were not instructed in the art of writing until they had shown that they knew the verses off by heart. Thus the texts were incised to the accompaniment of recitation. Many of the songs dealt with love and other matters of life and death; others were spells to save people in danger or to ensure good harvests or the fertility of their cattle. What has survived is mostly panegyrics of the islander's leaders, composed for special occasions. One kind of tablet, called *kohau o te ranga* was a sort of amulet that helped the wearer to overcome his enemies and included the text of prayers to the God, Rorai-hova.

The pupils of the *tangata rongo-rongo* were often their own sons or the most gifted children of the more eminent families. Every morning after the greeting, the call of *ko-koe-a*, the instructor checked the identities of those present to make sure there were no intruders.

The island's kings were mostly illiterate, but there were exceptions. One of these was King Ngaara, who lived in the first half of the nineteenth century. He took a great interest in the school and has passed into the history of the island as its enlightened master alive to the problems of the art and its teaching. He frequently visited the school, attended lessons and even personally examined the students. He was a strict examiner and blamed the instructors for every slip their pupils made. Once a year solemn competitions were organized, in which the best *tangata rongo-rongo* competed publicly reciting the texts of the tablets. Those who made mistakes were mocked unmercifully, while the winners were lavishly rewarded. The competition lasted several days and ended in a great banquet.

The island's hieroglyphic art achieved its apogee under King Ngaara and when he died, legend has it that his body was displayed on a catafalque of tablets of the "speaking wood" and he was then buried with them.

Unfortunately the last *tangata*, learned in the texts and writings, took the secrets of the *rongo-rongo* heiroglyphs with them to the grave.

ORIGINS OF THE EASTER ISLANDERS

Most of the attempts to explain the mysteries of Easter Island have been based on the premise that the splendid works of art encountered there were not the work of the people inhabiting the island at the time of its discovery. The island's advanced culture was thus attributed to an unknown people, on a high rung of the ladder of civilization and equipped with good technical means that were not known to the islanders of historical times. The sudden destruction of this previous civilization was attributed to some elemental catastrophe or perhaps to the landing of some barbarian warrior people.

These conjectures, however, are not borne out by the results of subsequent geological, archaeological or anthropological research.

At the moment there are three theories of the origins of Easter Island culture. According to the first, the originators were South American seamen who colonized the island in the fourth century AD. The second theory dates the beginning of Easter Island's civilization later and considers it Polynesian. The third theory has it that the island's civilization is a mixture of the influence of the early South American colonization and later (eleventh to fourteenth-century) Polynesian colonization.

At the present state of our knowledge, it must be admitted that the question remains open.

II

THE DUTCH DISCOVERERS

For a long time Admiral Jacob Roggeveen had been nervously pacing the cramped quarters of his cabin in his flag ship *Arend*. Finally he halted in front of a small cupboard let into the bulkhead, unlocked its stout iron padlock and from inside took out a large bundle of papers and with it resumed his seat at his desk. The papers, with which the Admiral was already familiar, contained the instructions given him by the West India Company as he had set sail from Amsterdam on 6th July 1721, almost a year before. The Company, not wishing to be left behind by its competitor, the East India Company, had despatched three ships: *Arend*, *Afrikaansche Galei* and *Thienhoven* under the command of Admiral Roggeveen, to sail round the world in search of the legendary southern continent — Terra Australis.

The Admiral's instructions, which he now knew almost by heart, were clear enough: he was to search for the southern continent in the region of Terra de Davis which had been sighted 35 years before (in 1687) by the crew of *Bachelor's Delight*, one of the ships of that famous English pirate, William Dampier. The Admiral's bundle of papers included the account of the sighting by the captain of *Bachelor's Delight*, Edward Davis, and her doctor, Lionel Wafer.

We steered South and by East, half Easterly, until we came to the Latitude of 27 Deg. 20 Min. S. when about two Hours before Day, we fell in with a small, low, sandy Island and heard a great roaring Noise, like that of the sea beating upon the Shore, right a head of the ship. Whereupon the Sailors, fearing to fall foul upon the Shore before Day, desired the Captain to put the Ship about, and to stand off till Day appeared; to which the Captain gave his consent. So we plied off till Day and then stood in without the guard of any Rocks. We stood in within a quarter of a Mile of the shore and could see it plainly; for 'twas a clear Morning, not foggy nor hazy. To the Westward, about 12 Leagues by Judgement, we saw a range of high Land, which we took to be

Islands, for there were several Partitions in the Prospect. This Land seem'd to reach about 14 or 16 Leagues in a Range, and there came thence great Flocks of Fowls. I, and many more of our Men would have made this Land and have gone ashore at it; but the Captain would not permit us. The small Island bears from Copayapo almost due E. 500 Leagues; and from the Gallapago's, under the Line, 600 Leagues.

From all this it was clear that the island Davis had sighted ought to be somewhere in those waters, yet it was already three weeks since the Dutchman had left their last call, the tiny island of Juan Fernandez off the coast of Chile, on 17th March 1722, sailing eastward and there had been no sight or sign of land since. The Admiral was becoming anxious. This voyage had already lasted nearly a year, during which time they had traversed the whole Atlantic Ocean from Holland to South America, successfully rounded the Horn and so far had come across no trace of that for which they were searching. Already they had sailed more than half way round the world.

The Admiral reached out across his desk for the large map of the world that lay there. This was dated 1675 and signed: Arent Roggeveen. This Arent Roggeveen was the admiral's father, in his day a famous mathematician and astronomer. In moments of difficulty or doubt, the Admiral would reach for his dead father's atlas. He it was who, nearly thirty years before, had made the first plans for discovering the unknown southern continent. Laying the atlas on his knees he let his finger follow the coastline of the great continent drawn as lying to the south of Africa and stretching from there to below South America and Java and named *Terra Australis Nondum Incognita* — the Southern Land so far Unknown.

Comforted by the feeling that he could not be far away from what he sought, the Admiral sat back in his chair and tired by the heat and pacing his cabin, he dozed off, despite the sounds coming from deck where the crew were noisily celebrating Easter Sunday.

An energetic knock on the door of his cabin abruptly roused the admiral. In response to his "Enter", the door opened and in came Jobon Koster, *Arend's* captain, his face alight with excitement.

"Admiral! Captain Rosendahl signals land on the horizon."

The admiral leaped from his chair and the two men hurried on deck. Through the telescope *Afrikaansche Galei* was clearly visible sailing far ahead of them. It was she had signalled having sighted land. The exciting news was passed back to Captain Bouman in *Thienhoven* sailing astern and then Roggeveen gave orders for both ships to close in with *Afrikaansche Galei*. There was little wind and to do this proved a lengthy manoeuvre.

When the three ships had finally closed within hailing distance, Captain Rosendahl was able to give the admiral particulars: how at a distance of five and a half miles to the southwest they could see a low island.

No one in the ships doubted but that the island was part of the coasts of the Southern Continent which, according to the atlas was to be found there and all were enormously delighted. Dusk was falling and the admiral ordered the three ships to anchor. He then retired to his cabin, where he again went to his cupboard, took out the great journal of the expedition and under 5th April 1722 made this entry: "We have given the name Paasch Eyland (Easter Island) to the new land in honour of its discovery on Easter Sunday."

The following day was fine and from dawn the crews of the three ships began preparing to sail round the coast of the island. A refreshing light breeze, just strong enough to fill the sails, favoured the undertaking. The ships sailed westwards at a distance of about ten miles so as to avoid running onto submerged rocks or reefs near the shore. At noon Admiral Roggeveen had them determine the island's geographical position: it was 27°4″ South and 265°42″ West. During the afternoon the three ships sailed slowly along the coast, one behind the other. Late that afternoon, the look-out in the crow's nest of the leading ship reported smoke on the port bow.

A moment or so later those on deck were also able to see a column of smoke rising from coastal heights, showing that the island was inhabited.

Roggeveen ordered the ships to heave-to level with the smoke-heights, while from *Arend* and *Thienhoven* ship's boats put out manned with well-armed sailors to take soundings and investigate the possibilities of landing at that point. As dusk began to fall the admiral recalled the boats and landing preparations were interrupted for the night. When the next day dawned it was drizzling to the accompaniment of rumbling thunder and frequent flashes of lightning that rent the darkly clouded sky. The wind, gusty and shifting, was not good for trying to land and the attempt was postponed.

Towards noon Captain Bouman's gig came alongside the Admiral's ship. An islander climbed agilely from the tossing little craft onto the ship's rail and jumped down on to the deck, where he was immediately surrounded by a throng of inquisitive sailors. He was young, muscular and well-built. His complexion was an olive brown and his features Polynesian. He was naked except for a few bits of glitter hung round his neck and from his ears.

"I've brought you a visitor, Sir," Captain Bouman told the Admiral who at that moment appeared on deck.

The Easter Islander seemed quite unafraid. He even tried to communicate with the sailors round him using sign language. It was the ship that seemed to interest him most: her masts, rigging, guns and navigational instruments. He went up to each object in turn, examined it carefully, touched it and appeared impressed.

The sailors were no less interested in the Easter Islander. After a little while a group appeared on deck with a large mirror from one of the cabins and this they set up against the mast. The islander went forward to examine the new object, but when he saw his reflection he halted in his tracks. Then he made various gestures and finally went round to the back of the mirror in search of his fellow islander.

When the islander had tired of the mirror-joke, the ship's orchestra assembled and began to play various lively tunes. The islander was evidently musical, for almost at once he began performing dance movements in perfect time, much to the delight of the crew.

Meanwhile Captain Bouman was telling the admiral how the islander had come out to *Thienhoven* in a small canoe. On board they had presented him with some pieces of material and tinsel and food, all of which, to the huge delight of the crew, he had hung round his neck — including a dried fish — and walked about thus proudly.

When the crew had had their enjoyment out of the islander, he was taken back in his canoe and dismissed with further presents: a string of blue beads, a small mirror, a pair of scissors and other trifles.

Back in his cabin Admiral Roggeveen again took out the Company's instructions and carefully compared Davis's account with his own observation and measurements, making notes on the edge of the document. The comparison put him in a good humour and taking out his own journal he wrote under the date-line 7th April 1722:

As we approached land at no great distance, we saw clearly that the description of it as a low, sandy island (as Captain William Dampier had described it, thus agreeing with Captain Davis and Lionel Wafer, whose log and other statements about the discovery Dampier had used largely in his own book) did not correspond at all with our discovery. This cannot be the land that these explorers stated extends for 14 to 16 miles of the field of vision as if it was a strip of elevated land, which according to Dampier's supposition, might be the extremity of an unknown southern land.

That 'Easter Island' cannot be then a sandy island is evident from the fact that their island was narrow and low, while Easter Island, on the contrary, measures 15 or 16 [Dutch] miles in circumference, has two high eminences with gently sloping sides, standing about 5 miles apart, with three or four other, smaller hills rising out of the plain round the bases of the other two, so that the land rises moderately above the level of the sea.

The main reason why at first, from a great distance, we thought this Easter Island to be sandy, was that we took dried grass and hay and dry or burned bushes, as barren ground, as from these outward appearances you could get the impression only of sparse, meagre vegetation.

In the light of the above one can conclude that the Easter Island we have discovered is different territory and farther to the east than the land which is one of the objectives of our expedition. Otherwise, its discoverers would have to accept with conviction a mass of lies in their written and verbal reports.*

The following day, after breakfast, boats put out from *Arend* and *Thienhoven*. Their crews, well armed, had been told to reconnoitre the shore, determine the number of islanders, their armament and strength and try to discover whether a landing might be resisted by force of arms and result in losses of men.

As the boats drew near the shore the men in them saw a crowd of islanders dressed in gay, multi-coloured garments. Some of the men said that they could see in their ears the glint of silver ornaments, shells and mother of pearl. Although the islanders made friendly gestures, as though encouraging their visitors to land, the Dutchmen rowed back to their ships in accordance with the orders they had been given not to land if they encountered islanders in any number.

Then, at sunset, the Admiral gave orders for the ships to approach and anchor a quarter of a mile off the eastern shore of the island.

* Roggeveen, Jacob: *Histoire d'Expedition de Trois Vaisseaux*. La Hage, 1739

As a result, by dawn the following day, the sea round the ships was alive with the islanders' little canoes, the latter not sharing the Europeans' mistrust and caution. Instead, they climbed up on deck with the utmost agility and swarmed all over the ships, poking their noses into everything and looking at everything with the greatest interest. The Dutchmen were bewildered by this bloodless conquest of their ships by a horde of swarthy "Indians", as they called them and their embarrassment emboldened the islanders to the extent that they began appropriating little things that took their fancy. They even went so far as to pull the caps and hats off the heads of the phlegmatic Dutchmen and jump over the rail into the water with their booty. Obviously there was no question of recovering the things the islanders took, especially as the islanders were superb swimmers, many of them swimming out to the ships in the first place. Their impertinence grew and one islander climbed from his canoe straight through the porthole into the cabin of the captain of *Afrikaansche Galei*, pulled the cloth off the table and wrapping it round himself escaped the way he had come. As night began to fall the islanders went back to their island and peace returned to the ships.

Admiral Roggeveen now decided to return the islanders' visit. For the landing he selected 134 of the bravest of his men and early in the morning of 10th April three long boats and a number of other boats were lowered into the water and the men, armed with muskets, pistols and cutlasses, climbed down into them. Using the utmost caution, keeping close together, they landed on the sandy shore, leaving twenty well-armed sailors to protect the boats and cover a possible withdrawal to them with two canonades mounted in the boat from *Afrikaansche Galei*.

The reason for this caution was that they knew of what had befallen the Dutch fleet under Nassau a short time before, when too much trust in the Indians of Tierra del Fuego had cost the lives of seventeen Europeans.

Every precaution was maintained as they marched inland in three columns, maintaining military formation, headed by the captains of the ships. They endeavoured by signs to make the Indians who thronged round them maintain a respectable distance, but their gestures did not always have the desired effect. At one point the throng was so great that it was difficult to keep moving at all. Then, to everyone's surprise, especially Roggeveen's, five shots were heard from the rear of the column

and a voice shouted:
"High time, too! Fire!"

Then followed a score or so more shots. The islanders
scattered in terror leaving on the grass ten or twelve dead and
a dozen or so wounded. The officers intervened before there
could be further shooting, calming the agitated sailors and
categorically forbidding anyone to fire at the fleeing islanders.
The Admiral at once set about discovering the person
responsible for this provocative and unnecessary shooting.
This proved to be the assistant pilot of *Thienhoven* who with six
men was acting as rear guard. According to him one of the
islanders had seized the barrel of his carbine and tried to wrest
it from him. Another had tried to pull the coat off one of the
sailors in the column. When the sailors began hitting the
islanders, the latter withdrew a short distance but began
stoning the sailors and it was then the assistant pilot had given
the order to fire. Obviously there was no time to go into the
accident more fully or to hear other people's versions and,
repeating his orders that there was to be no shooting, the
Admiral ordered the column to move on.

The result of this unfortunate incident surprised the
Dutchmen. Shortly afterwards a delegation headed by an old
man who appeared to be a chief, came to the admiral. He
listened to the explanation given by the Dutchmen in sign
language: that the shooting had been an accident caused by
an aggressive throwing of stones and that the Dutchmen had
no intention of harming the islanders, but wanted to be friends
with them. Apparently this was understood and accepted, for
shortly afterwards a further delegation appeared bringing the
astonished Dutchmen baskets full of gifts, mainly fruit,
vegetables, poultry, sugar cane, spices and birds. The
Dutchmen, however, would not accept the gifts, but bought 60
birds and 30 bunches of bananas for which they paid with
linen which delighted the islanders.

Once the islanders had become more accustomed to the
sight of the strangers and were no longer thronging round
them so tightly, the Dutchmen were able to look round and
get some idea of the island and its people. Unfortunately they
stayed there so short a time that the information provided by
Roggeveen is meagre, in places inaccurate and even obviously
false.

Various details of the islanders' clothing particularly
interested the Dutchmen. According to Roggeveen they wore
three or four folds of a brightly coloured cloth of vegetable

origin. Its yellowish colour proved to be very impermanent, coming off not only from new, freshly coloured pieces of the material, but even from clothing that had been worn for a considerable time.

What interested the Dutch most, however, was the islanders' characteristic ear-ornaments, which were so striking that even the sailors in the boats reconnoitring the island from quite a distance had noticed them. What the latter had supposed to be large silver earrings, proved not to be metal, but made of the root of some unidentified plant and either round or oval with a diameter of one or two inches.

In order to accommodate these silver-coloured discs, the lobes of the islanders' ears were stretched from early childhood, so that those of some of them hung almost to their shoulders. If the possessor of such long ears was doing anything in which his long lobes were getting in his way, he simply hooked the lobes over the tips of his ears to keep them out of the way, which looked rather peculiar.

The islanders were tall, muscular, well-built, swarthy and some had painted their skins blue. Their teeth were dazzlingly white and even those of the old were sound and healthy. The Dutch were also impressed by the strength of the islanders' teeth, for they cracked the hardest nuts with them with apparent ease.

Most of the islanders had short hair and beards, though a few wore their hair plaited into a pigtail like the Chinese.

The Dutch encountered few women, especially young ones, and this they put down to male jealousy, presuming the islanders to have hidden them away. The older women they came across were dressed in nothing but a piece of cloth wound round their hips and reaching to above the knee.

The Dutch were interested in the islanders' religious beliefs, but did not stay long enough to discover details, though they noticed that the islanders placed burning lamps and offerings in front of huge stone statues, kneeling and falling on their faces before them. The Dutch were intrigued by these statues, yet they did not find time to examine them.

At first we were amazed by these stone figures, [Roggeveen wrote] because we could not understand how a people that did not have hard, stout timber could have raised them, to say nothing of the strong ropes needed to build the hoists necessary to raise the statues, some of which were a good thirty feet high and wide in proportion. Our wonder diminished, however, when on removing a piece of stone we discovered that the statue was moulded of clay or a kind of 'fat' earth and then covered with small pieces of stone set close together giving the impression of human figures. What is more, one could see falling from the shoulders flat surfaces representing hands, so that the whole depicted a figure with garments flowing from the neck to the feet. On the heads the figures had tall baskets filled with stones painted white.

That was the total extent of the admiral's account of the statues given in his description of the voyage. Since then the island he discovered has become world-famous because of them. It is obvious that Roggeveen did not himself take a closer look at the statues which are carved out of solid blocks of volcanic lava; at least none of the later explorers of Easter Island came across any "clay" statues such as Roggeveen described.

One of the mysteries the Dutch tried to elucidate was how the islandeers prepared their food. Nowhere could the Dutchmen see pots, pans or other kitchen vessels. It transpired that the islanders dug shallow holes in the ground, lined these with stones and then made fires of dried grasses to heat the stones — not having wood — and cooked their food over the hot stones. The Dutchmen were full of praise for the method, asserting that the poultry they were given prepared in this way was delicious, clean and hot.

Roggeveen, remembering other people's experiences elsewhere in the world, never lost his fear of being ambushed throughout their brief stay at the island. He kept a tight rein on his men who were not allowed to roam about the island. This order proved unnecessary, as the islanders behaved in the most friendly manner to their visitors.

Some of the Dutchmen did visit the islanders' homes, which Roggeveen describes thus:

> Their houses and cottages are free of embellishment. They measure some fifty feet long by fifteen feet wide and some nine feet high. As we could see from the houses recently erected the walls are made of stakes driven into the ground and strengthened with transverse poles, which are covered with long cloths to a height of four or five feet, the gaps between them being filled with a kind of long root or grass pressed in tight and knotted on the outside (with a cord made of a plant called *piet* and just as good as our twist). Thanks to this, their houses are just as well protected against wind and rain as if covered with Dutch thatch.
>
> These houses have only one entrance, so low that in order to enter the islanders must go on their hands and knees or bend

double. Entrance and roof are semi-circular. All the dwellings we
saw (these long buildings had nothing to admit light but the
entrance opening) had mats on the floor and oblong stones used
as pillows. In addition, round the walls, stand large round hewn
stones about three or four feet in diameter, washed and cleaned.
In our opinion these served as seats when the cool evenings keep
the people indoors.

Finally, it must be stated that the dwelling houses, of which we
saw no more than six or seven in the place where we landed, are
used in common. Their large dimensions and the fact that there
are so few indicate that large numbers live and sleep together in
each building. If one is to conclude from this that the women are
shared among them, one would expect quarrels and squabbling to
result.

Another thing that aroused the Dutchmen's professional
interest was the boats used by the islanders and their
equipment. These boats were fragile, wretched little craft only
nine or ten feet long. Built of light strips of wood tied together
with fibre they let in the water and the islanders evidently did
not know how to make them water-tight, for they expended
more energy baling them than in rowing.

The chief of the islanders hospitably invited the Dutchmen
to visit the other side of the island where, he gave them to
understand, were the fields and plantations where had grown
the fruit and vegetables presented to them. Although they
would have liked to get to know more of the island, the
Admiral was feeling apprehensive because of the strong
northerly wind that got up. He was afraid lest high waves
should swamp and sink his boats, which were laden to the
gunwale with heavily-armed sailors, on the way back, so he
ordered a return to the ships and they took farewell of the
islanders.

Back on board the Admiral at once ordered sail to be set
and the ships headed west, not wanting to remain offshore
with high seas and gusty winds. In accordance with his
instructions the Admiral made another attempt to find the
sandy little island described by Wafer. Not doing so, he noted
in his journal:

   I have nothing more to say beyond that those three (Dampier,
Davis and Wafer) who were Engligh, were as free with the truth as
they were with the treasure of the Spaniards.

Sticking to his instructions Roggeveen sailed west heading
for the islands of the Dutch East Indies, where an unpleasant

surprise awaited him. When, on 10th December 1722, the ships put into the port of Batavia, Roggeveen was arrested at the request of the Dutch East India Company which then controlled the territory and employed these methods to defeat its competitors, the Dutch West India Company which Roggeveen represented. The admiral and his companions were eventually shipped back home, but only after a trial and several months' imprisonment.

III

THE CONQUISTADORS IN THE PACIFIC

Early in 1770 a courier from Madrid presented himself at the viceregal palace in Lima. Among the letters he brought the viceroy, Don Manuel de Amat, was one from the Minister of State for Indian Affairs, Don Julian De Arriaga, which contained disquieting news of increasing activity on the part of the English and French in the Southern Pacific. There had been further cases of lands previously discovered and occupied by the Spaniards being wrested from them. The subjects of the king of Spain in the powerful colonial empire of Central and Southern America, though irritated by the English corsairs' sudden attacks on ports and towns, did not feel that these constituted any particular threat. The situation, however, was much worse on the other side of the great ocean where, in 1762, the English had taken Manila, capital of Spain's Asiatic possessions, and were now threatening her Philippine possessions more and more seriously.

Madrid was now planning much closer links between Spain's possessions which lay scattered about the vast expanses of the globe, in the hope that their combined forces might withstand the growing power of England and France, which were proving more and more aggressive. Because of the huge distances between the American and Asiatic coasts of the Pacific it was not enough merely to enlarge the fleet. The ships that were to maintain liaison between these distant possessions would need permanent bases where they could take refuge in the event of danger and obtain provisions and water if they had been unduly long at sea. This had prompted the idea of establishing a chain of naval bases to link Spain's American and Asiatic possessions and this, in turn, called for considerable exploration of those as yet scarcely explored parts of the vast ocean.

According to the ideas prevailing then, somewhere in the Southern Pacific betwen Asia and South America, lay the unknown land: Terra Australis Incognita. So far, however, all search for it had been vain, the only result having been the discovery of numerous small islands and archipelagos. Madrid now thought that these Polynesian islands might help the realization of its plans.

The letter sent to Don Julian told him that the king, Charles III, was entrusting to his Viceroy the task of extending the Spanish dominion in the eastern part of the Pacific. Further, the Viceroy was to organize expeditions to discover and annex David's Island* which was marked on the maps west of the American coast though no one had seen it for almost fifty years. The Viceroy was urged to lose no time over this in case the English or French got there ahead of him. The need for hurry was stressed by the news that in 1764 Byron and Wallis had looked for and failed to find the island, while, two years later, a Frenchman, Bougainville, had similarly failed as had another Englishman, Carter, in 1767.

What the explorers in the Pacific were looking for above all was what had brought Columbus to the coasts of America two and a half centuries before: the sea road westward to China and India. There was, indeed, no time to lose.

The first and most important thing, that on which the success of the venture would largely depend, was the choice of leader for the expedition. Don Manuel's choice was an experienced sailor, a man of nearly seventy, Don Felipe Gonzales y Haedo, who had arrived in Callao de Lima only a couple of weeks previously with the *San Lorenzo* which had brought fresh troops and supplies for the garrison in Lima, after taking six months on the voyage from Cadiz. A few days previously the Viceroy had had the pleasure of delivering to Don Felipe a document sent out from Spain, the patent promoting him to "Capitan de Navio". Don Felipe came from a renowned though impoverished noble family and the Viceroy had heard nothing but praise of him, especially of his skill as a navigator acquired in half a century of sailing the seas and oceans of the world. This, then, was the man the Viceroy summoned to his palace and entrusted with the command of the expedition. Don Felipe chose for his second ship, the frigate *Santa Rosalia* commanded by another experienced sailor, Don Antonio Domonte, who was similarly promoted to Capitan de Navio a fortnight after joining the expedition.

*All the Spanish documents call it David's Island, though the description and its position leave no doubt that it is Davis's Island which is meant. The name must have been wrongly transcribed and the mistake never corrected. Spanish sources make no mention of the voyages and discoveries of the Dutch.

The preparations took several months, but in October 1770 all was ready and on the tenth of that month the two ships, *San Lorenzo* and *Santa Rosalia*, set sail from Callao in Peru heading south-west.

The first month of the voyage passed uneventfully, then in the afternoon of 9th November, the faint outline of land* was observed from the leading ship. The following day there were black petrels and other birds the Spaniards did not recognize flying about both ships, a sure sign of land being near. On 14th November Don Felipe summoned Don Antonio and the other officers of *Santa Rosalia* aboard *San Lorenzo* for a conference. He then told them that although according to Don Felipe's instructions it was not anticipated that they should start their search before the 264th meridian, the signs they now had of land being near had decided him that they ought to continue sailing west. This was agreed unanimously and the officers returned to their duties.

The further west the two ships sailed, the greater became the number and variety of birds round them, and finally, early in the morning of 15th November 1770, the Spaniards caught sight of the rocky coast of an island which they felt must be the David's Island for which they were searching. It was, indeed, Easter Island which the Dutch had been the first to visit half a century before. By noon of that day the two ships reached the island and sailed northwards along the coast looking for a bay in which they might land. Later in the afternoon they saw three columns of smoke rising from the shore. The three fires appeared equidistant from each other and the Spaniards took this to be a signal to them from the islanders, of whom, however, they could see no sign. It was some time later that they saw a group of about eighteen people walking along the crest of a high eminence. Through the telescope the Spaniards could see that some of these were dressed in long coats like Indian ponchos. At first glance they reminded the Spaniards of European soldiers in their cloaks. Discovering to their relief that that was not what they were, the Spaniards then saw that some of the others were naked and some wore head-dresses of plumes. The colourful group then sat down on the crest, as though to hold council, while the ships sailed on. Later that afternoon, they came to a bay which at first glance looked as though it were suitable for landing. Both ships sent boats away to take soundings. Not knowing the attitude of the

*Probably the reef known as Sala y Gomez which lies east of Easter Island.

islanders to Europeans, the crews of both boats were heavily armed and instructed to exercise the utmost caution. As the boats approached the shore, the Spaniards saw on the beach a group of islanders, their naked bodies brightly painted, shouting and gesturing to them.

As the bay proved to be shallow and unsuitable for large ships and also as darkness was falling, it was decided to postpone landing until the following day, so the two ships anchored off shore. Early on 16th November *San Lorenzo* lowered a boat. In it was a contingent of officers and men, seamen and provisions for six days. Their instructions were to land, explore the interior and discover the attitude of the islanders to strangers. The islanders, bolder than on the previous day, were crowding the beach and greeted the Spaniards noisily, though amiably. The Spaniards, though taking every precaution, made the islanders trifling presents of small metal crosses, pieces of clothing, food and tobacco. These were received rapturously, and the islanders appeared to find salt pork and rice delicious.

Having thus ascertained that the islanders were amicably disposed, the Spaniards began to explore the interior of the island. Their attention was at once attracted by the huge statues standing on the hillsides. They realized that these were of stone and this filled them with admiration for the islanders and their skill and artistry. When they became better acquainted with the kindly, but primitive islanders, the Spaniards began to doubt whether they were in fact the authors of the statues. One of the Spanish officers has thus described the impression the huge statues made on them:

We discovered that what we had first thought to be bushes of conical shape were really statues or carvings of the gods to which the islanders prayed. They are of stone and of such height and girth that they look like huge pillars. And I was later to discover when examining and measuring them that each is a whole made of one block, only the crown or head-covering being separate. In the top of the head-covering is a slight hollow in which the bones of the dead are placed. One may thus conclude that the statues are both idols and tombs. It is, however, difficult to see how the islanders have been able to raise these huge columns and keep them balanced on the quantity of small stones of which the foundations and base are made. The material out of which these statues are carved is stone, hence their great weight. I gave one a blow with a pick-axe and sparks flew, which was proof of how hard it was. The crown was made of a different sort of stone,

(*above*) Easter Islanders on the deck of a European Ship; (*below*) Easter Island women and European sailors on the shore—drawings made by members of the early expeditions

Sketches of the Easter Island statues made by members of the
nineteenth-century expeditions

which is plentiful, but I never came across stone of the kind of which the statues are made. The carving of the statues is very rough. The only features of the face are simple cavities for the eyes; the nostrils are only just indicated, but the lips run from ear to ear in a horizontal groove. There is a certain resemblance to a neck, but no hands or feet. From the shoulders down, the statues are a straight, shapeless trunk. The section of the head-covering is considerably larger than the head on which it rests, the lower edge protruding well beyond the forehead, which ensures that it does not fall. I was able to discover this when examining one of the smaller statues that had a sort of bung rising from it, carved in such a way that its shape and dimensions fitted the hole or joint hollowed in the corresponding crown. This arrangement ensures that the crown rests firmly on the head and prevents it falling. One cannot help wondering how these people who have no machines or tools for building, have been able to raise these crowns or head-coverings to the height of such tall columns. I even suspect that the stone of which these columns are made is not native to the island, which has no iron, hemp or timber. There is much to be elucidated.*

The Spaniards carefully investigated the statues despite the fact that the islanders made no secret of their displeasure at having strangers examining the statues they worshipped and which in their language they called *moai*. There was another kind of figure or idol, some of which the author of the above also described. These were clothed and portable. Some twelve feet long, they were really Judas figures stuffed with straw or hay. They had hands and feet; the heads had primitive eyes, noses and lips and tufts of black hair made of rushes falling down for half the length of the trunk. On certain days these idols were brought to the islanders' meeting places and, judging by the organized ceremonies, the Spaniards concluded that these so-called *copeca* were used in entertainment.

The Spaniards, of course, were mainly interested in the islanders as potential subjects of the King of Spain. Their accounts reflect their disappointment at finding the Easter Islanders so poor and wretched. They saw no evidence of ornaments made of gold, silver or, indeed, any metal, to say nothing of precious stones, such as in those days European travellers bought in quantities for worthless tinsel or simply

---

*Gonzalez y Haedo Felipe: *The Voyage of Captain Felipe Gonzalez in the ship of the line San Lorenzo with the frigate Santa Rosalia in Company to Easter Island, in 1770-1771* (1908)

stole from conquered peoples.

The Spaniards were surprised by the type of people they found in the island, for these resembled Europeans far more closely than did the Indians or Polynesians. They measured two of the tallest: one was 1.99 metres, the other 1.95 metres. Many of the men wore beards.

Gonzalez y Haedo Felipe wrote in his account:

> Their physiognomy in no way reminds one of the continental Indians of Chile, Peru or New Spain. The colour of their skins varies from white through swarthy to reddish. They do not have flat noses nor thick lips and their hair is short and chestnut coloured: only some have black hair, that of others has a reddish or cinnamon tinge. They are tall, well-built and of good proportions. There are no cripples, hunchbacks, bandy-legged or otherwise deformed.
>
> Their appearance gives a pleasant impression and reminds one more of the European than of the Indian. Judging by their quickness and intelligence I think they would be easy to tame and convert to whatever religion was put before them.

The Spaniards, who used both the cross and the sword to build their empire, did not forget their Christian mission of saving souls even in this out-of-the-way island. So they had taken with them priests, though owing to the shortness of their stay at the island, these had no opportunity to start work. Later, after the expedition had been concluded, towards the end of 1771, the King of Spain told the Viceroy of Peru to send priests and missionaries to Easter Island to convert and baptize the islanders, but fortunately for the latter the Viceroy had more important things to worry about at the time and did not do so, with the result that the Easter Islanders escaped the benefits of the Spanish Inquisition and were spared the fate of the American Indians.

Encouraged by the presents they received, more and more islanders went out to the Spanish ships. The island being treeless and quite bare, the speed with which presents and the many objects the islanders stole disappeared without trace, suggested that the islanders must have secret, subterranean hiding-places. Another thing the Spaniards noticed was the complete absence of children. It was as if the population consisted solely of adult males and a few very frivolous women.

The martial Spaniards were sarcastic about the peaceable nature of the inhabitants who, as they noticed, had no weapons of any kind. Intrigued by the scars on some of the islanders' hands, the Spaniards asked how they had come by them and were told that they were the results of accidents and caused by the sharp stone tools that the islanders used. To test them, one of the Spaniards produced a bow and arrows and handed them to one of the islanders whose hands were covered with scars. To the delight of his fellows, the islander hung the bow round his neck and proudly wore it thus in complete ignorance of its real use. When other islanders did the same with the daggers and swords the Spaniards gave them, the Spaniards decided it was no use trying to educate the islanders in knightly skills. The islanders, however, proved remarkably good linguists, learning to use Spanish phrases with astounding quickness. Thus by the time they returned to the ships the Spaniards had taught them to say *Ave Maria* and *Long live the king, King of Spain* and felt that they had done their patriotic duty.

The following day so many islanders swarmed aboard the two ships that, as a safety precaution, the Spaniards had to ask them to leave.

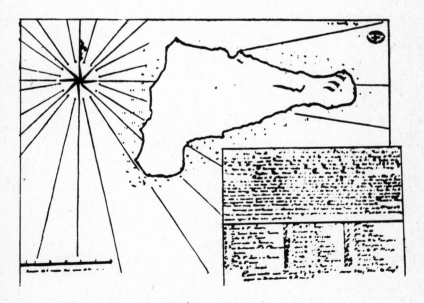

Map of Easter Island made by the Spanish expedition of 1770

During their stay the Spaniards sailed all round the island mapping its coast and giving Spanish names to individual places. Theirs was the first map of the island — and a reasonably accurate one — which was a real contribution to our knowledge of Easter Island. They found that the island was not large, being about fifty miles round. Nowhere did they find a bay into which ships could put. On the contrary, the whole coastline was steep, rocky and the inshore water full of treacherous reefs and dangerously submerged rocks.

This circumnavigation of the island allowed the Spaniards to become better acquainted with the islanders and their way of life, for they stopped at a number of points, always sending a boat ashore, the crew of which quickly made contact with the islanders. These were all of the same race, had the same culture and the same habits as those they had encountered when they first landed. Indeed, they had the same tendency to purloin things, as the Spaniards did not fail to mention in their accounts of the voyage.

During the evening of 17th November one of the ships anchored at the mouth of a small bay that looked relatively calm and tranquil and almost the entire crew went ashore with food intending to cook themselves a hot meal. Within a short time a crowd of islanders appeared bringing with them armfuls of fruit and chickens. Don Cayetano de Langara, who was in command, gave orders that no one was to accept anything from the islanders unless he paid for it. They did buy a certain amount of fresh food. Then, when the Spaniards were ready to eat, they discovered to their surprise that the islanders had all vanished, except for one who remained as though on watch. He, however, ate the pork and rice the Spaniards gave him with evident relish.

Having finished their meal the Spaniards went for a walk inland and there met the islanders who had vanished so mysteriously. They came forward in the most friendly way and conducted the Spaniards to their long, very low dwelling house, which was built in six columns and had only the one low entrance. It looked as though the inhabitants of this strange village did not have separate homes, but lived together in a sort of indeterminate community. Round about were small gardens and plantations in which the Spaniards recognized sugar cane, sweet potatoes, yams, white pumpkin among other plants they did not know.

Nowhere did they see any animals, whether domestic or wild, except chickens and rats. They saw only delicate bushy

figs so different from the fig the Spaniards knew that they
scarcely recognized them. Their identification was supported
by the dried figs later given them by the islanders, the native
name for which was *gecoy*. The Spaniards noted a complete
absence of birds and insects. Only small numbers of sea birds
nested on the coastal cliffs, while there was not a bird to be seen
inland. Having shown the Europeans their village, the
hospitable islanders began singing and dancing which was
taken as a display of their friendly feeling towards the
newcomers.

As they walked about the island, the Spaniards discovered
the solution to the mystery of the sudden appearances and
disappearances of the islanders, who almost seemed to appear
out of the ground, or vanish into it. It turned out that most of
the islanders lived in underground caverns or caves in the
rocks, the entrances to which were so narrow and
inconvenient that some had to crawl in feet first.

The leaders stood out from the rest of the islanders. They
were mostly older men to whom the others showed respect.
Some of these leaders lived in the long houses already
described, others, those whom the Spaniards called priests,
lived near the statues in little houses made of stone.

The Spaniards completed their circumnavigation of Easter
Island on 19th November, on which day there was a tropical
down-pour. The ships were anchored in the bay where the
first landing had been made. The evening and most of the
night were spent in preparing for the ceremony of taking
possession of the island in the name of the king of Spain
planned for the following day.

The new day dawned fresh and clear after the downpour
and the Spaniards at once began landing the officers, crews
and soldiers involved. This was quite an undertaking as there
were more than 250 pecple to be conveyed in a few small
boats.

Once all were ashore, to the accompaniment of a tattoo,
they set off inland in a colourful procession headed by two
priests in black, followed by men carrying three wooden
crosses which were to be set up on the tops of three hills in the
north-easterly part of the island. Some time after this strange
procession had moved off, the omnipresent, inquisitive
islanders began to appear. As gay and obliging as ever, they
relieved the Spaniards of the heavy crosses and carried them
for them. The farther they went, the more their numbers
increased, dancing and singing as they accompanied the

Spaniards uphill. When the priests began singing the litany and psalms the quick-witted islanders joined in with "*ora pro nobis*" in such a good Latin accent that the Spaniards were surprised.

Half an hour later the procession finally reached its objective. Again the islanders hastened to help the Spaniards who were fatigued by their long walk, and eagerly began digging holes for the crosses to stand in. As one of these was being dug a spring of good water gushed, which the Spaniards took as a good omen.

When the holes had been dug, the crosses were erected and three salutes fired from muskets which were answered by twenty-one salvos from the guns in the ships. The assembled Spaniards seven times shouted *Viva el Rey* which the islanders caught and echoed and this ended the ceremony of taking possession of the island, which was solemnly named San Carlos, after the king. The date was 20th November, 1770.

To legalize the act, the islanders who were there were invited to sign a document transferring sovereignty over their island to the Spanish crown. The delighted islanders, who had helped so eagerly throughout the ceremony, were as quick to pick up the pen and place strange signatures at the foot of the

'Signatures' of the leaders of Easter Island appended to the 'treaty' with Spain, 1770

document. These signatures are deceptively like the hieroglyphs found in various other parts of the world. The document has been preserved to this day.

The following day the Spaniards, conscious of having done their job well, raised anchor and sailed away with all sail set, leaving their king's new subjects behind for ever, as it proved; for they never returned.

IV

ENGLISH SEAMEN AND THE MYSTERIOUS ISLE

For the last year and a half two British ships, *Resolution* (462 tons) and *Adventure* (326 tons) had been sailing the waters of the southern hemisphere as they vainly searched for the legendary Terra Incognita of the south. Here, England was competing with the younger colonial powers, France and Holland, and as the Admiralty attached great importance to the search, it had put Captain James Cook in command of the expedition. Cook left Plymouth for what was to be the second circumnavigation of the globe on 13th June 1772. His plan was to sail round the world along the highest possible southern latitude in the hope of finding the southern continent. As more and more expeditions sent out for this purpose returned without having achieved their aim, the area of search was gradually moved farther and farther south of the equator almost into the Antarctic. This led to the discovery of Australia and a number of the archipelagos and islands of Polynesia, but so far no one had come across the legendary land which most geographers of the day thought must lie in the area of the South Pole and be of a size to counterbalance the continents of the northern hemisphere.

This search for the southern continent took Captain Cook's expedition into the waters of the Antarctic Ocean, so that its members were the first people in history to cross the antarctic circle thus getting closer to the South Pole than anyone had before. During December 1773 and January 1774, the southern hemisphere's summer, the expedition sailed in the direction of the yet undiscovered Antarctica, turning back only when ice made further progress to the south impossible. These weeks spent sailing among ice in the antarctic climate weakened the crews with the result that signs of scurvy, the plague of all expeditions in those days, began to appear.

To make matters worse, on 25th February 1774, Cook himself was laid low by a severe infection of the gall bladder and had to hand over the command to his first officer, Cooper.

Fortunately, Cook's condition began to improve a couple of days later, though whether that was due to Dr Patten's attentions or the toughness of Cook's constitution, we do not know. Indeed, it may have been the salutary effect of the broth of fresh meat specially prepared for the captain by Forster, the expedition's naturalist, to make which he sacrificed his beloved dog, which thus became the first victim of scurvy or, rather, of the threat of it. In those days the cause of scurvy, a lack of vitamins, was still unknown — as, of course, were vitamins. All that was known was that fresh meat, vegetables and fruit had a curative and prophylactic effect. Under the threat of scurvy Cook ordered all sail to be set for the North, hoping to reach one of the Polynesian islands and there allow his exhausted crew to defeat the dread disease and recuperate in the good southern climate.

On 1st March 1774, at eight in the morning, the look-out in the *Resolution's* crow's nest sighted land to the west. Informed of this, Cook realized that this must be Easter Island and he gave orders to prepare to land. They spent all day searching the rocky coast for a suitable place where the ships might lie at anchor. Dusk had fallen before they could do so and so it was decided to postpone landing until the following day, the ships hanging about off a place where a wide gentle curve of sandy coast looked as though it formed an inlet or a bay.

Early the next morning a small boat with two men in it was observed coming out to the ships from this sandy stretch. Paddling hard the two men quickly covered the mile separating the shore from the ships. When they came alongside the two islanders made friendly gestures and held up a bunch of bananas which was quickly hoisted aboard, whereupon the islanders paddled back to the island. The English took this as a proof of the peaceable disposition of the islanders and that here they might find the rest they all needed after the fatigues of sailing in the Antarctic. As the ships were sailing along the coast — they went as far as the northern headland — another islander suddenly appeared on deck of one of the ships. He at once began measuring the length of the ship. Amazed, the Englishmen watched him carefully counting the feet from bows to stern and realized that in doing so he was using the same names for the numerals as they had heard used by the natives on Otaheite. However, when they tried talking to the Easter Islander in the tongue of Otaheite, he did not understand.

Meanwhile a throng of islanders had gathered on the shore.

From the ships they could see that these were completely unarmed. Nobody was even holding a stick. They seemed most inquisitive and made friendly gestures to the Europeans. Cook ordered boats to be lowered and, getting into one, was rowed towards the shore. The impatient islanders were unable to wait and, jumping in, swam out to meet the boats. Having disembarked, the English tried by gestures to tell the islanders that they wished to buy supplies. To encourage them, the English distributed some tinsel and a moment later people appeared with sweet potatoes, plantains and sugar canes which they bartered for nails, glass and clothing. Like the other Europeans before them, the English now discovered that they were dealing with true artists in the crafts of purloining and trickery. Before they realized the fact, they had lost a number of small objects. Not content with these, the islanders became so importunate that it was all the English could do to prevent them removing the hats off their heads and taking things from their pockets.

Shortly before leaving England Captain Cook had been told of the Spaniards' recent visit to Easter Island and now saw evidence of it in the dress of several of the islanders, one of whom was wearing an European hat on his head, another was stalking about in a long coat, while others were wearing red silk gloves on their hands. While they were bartering, a man suddenly appeared and, shouting, drove the throng away. Judging by his gestures he was the owner of the plantation of sweet potatoes beside which they were and that it was his potatoes the islanders in their eagerness to barter, were handing out. Thus the islanders not only had a peculiar attitude to the property of foreigners, but were not above stealing from each other.

Being still weak after his illness, Cook remained on the beach with a few of his men, sending just a small detachment inland to reconnoitre. They, too, found the island quite barren, treeless and with only a few scattered plantations of potatoes and sugar cane.

Shortly after setting off inland the little company encountered another islander, a middle-aged man tattooed from head to foot and with his face painted white. In one hand he held a stick with a white rag hanging from the end. With a gesture of authority he dismissed the other islanders and, putting himself at the head of the little company, they continued on towards the village. The road led through what must have been the most fertile part of the island with plots of tilled ground and plantations. The inhabitants of the various villages welcomed the foreigners with gifts of baked potatoes and sugar cane, thrusting them into the hands of each in turn as they filed along the narrow path. While these were giving gifts, others were trying to rob the foreigners even of the food their compatriots had just given them. One of the islanders became so bold that he seized a large basket from the English and ran off with it. The sailors fired at him and bowled him over making him let go of the basket. A moment later he got up and suddenly vanished. They never saw him again, so they never discovered whether he had been badly wounded or only superficially, or even whether he had survived his encounter with the English.

The incident caused a certain confusion. Disquieted, the islanders thronged round their leader gesticulating and apparently asking what to do. The leader, however, calmly unfurled his white 'flag', made the crowd move aside and conducted the company further on its way.

It was a long march to the western part of the island and when they reached it, the English were delighted to see a spring. They were then well above sea level and the water was sweet and delicious. Unfortunately, closer examination showed that it was also incredibly dirty and polluted. It was not long before they discovered the cause. They watched in amazement as the islanders queued up and, one by one, stepped into the middle of the pool, drank a tiny quantity and then washed himself all over. That done, he stepped out, making way for the next.

The Englishmen's attention was particularly taken by the stone statues, which had previously so intrigued the Dutch and the Spaniards. They had first encountered them down by the coast and now discovered that there were others inland. In the western part of the island they saw three stone pedestals, or rather the ruins of them. Once four huge statues had stood on each. Now, on two of them all the statues had been overthrown and damaged or broken into pieces; on the third, however, only one statue had been toppled. The English measured the platforms and the statues, one of which was 32½ feet tall and ten feet across. Despite the fact that in those latitudes objects do not throw much of a shadow at two o'clock in the afternoon, the group of thirty Englishmen were able to sit in the shade of just one of these statues.

The fact that some of the statues had been overthrown and broken made the English conclude that a previous visit by

Europeans had led to some outburst or quarrel which had resulted in their destruction. Cook's men made a close examination of several pedestals. What impressed them most was the discovery that these were made of huge blocks of stone, cut and dressed with such exactitude that they held together without the use of mortar of any kind. The excellence of the mason's work made Cook suspect that it could not have been performed by the present race of islanders nor their ancestors, but rather by some people of unusual intelligence and high technical accomplishment, who perhaps had inhabited the islands many hundreds of years before. Who were they? What had become of them? Why had they died out, if they had such a high level of civilization? There was no answer as far as Cook and his men could discover.

In Cook's opinion the islanders he encountered could have had little in common with this mysterious people, if only because they made no attempt to repair the ravages of time on the pedestals, probably because they did not know how and did not have the tools, for the English certainly did not see any.

With Cook was a Polynesian called Mahine whom he had brought from Tahiti. It turned out that Mahine was able to make himself understood to some extent and through him the English learned that the statues were not idols nor images of gods, but funeral monuments to the arikis, as the members of the sacred royal family of the island were called. This was borne out in part by the pieces of skeletons and human bones found round the foundations. The number of these led the English to suppose that the pedestals were used as tombs by the present inhabitants of the island. Some of the latter, who were present when the English were examining the platforms, tried to explain in sign language that many of those buried there had gone to heaven.

The women the English encountered wore peculiar hats of plaited grass as depicted in Hodge's drawings. Apart from these the islanders' garb was unusually meagre. Their eagerness to acquire European garments: hats, trousers, shirts or any scrap of material — was such as made them steal. Those who were less adroit and cunning tried to acquire these longed-for objects by way of honest barter. When they realized that the Europeans had had enough of the few kinds of food they were able to offer them, they began producing their own manufactures. These consisted mostly of plaited hats, feather headdresses, necklaces, ear-ornaments and small wooden

carvings of human figures. These last particularly interested
the learned members of the expedition. Each was a miniature
work of art. Unlike the coarse stone statues, these little
wooden figures of people of both sexes were delicately carved
and beautifully polished. They were between twelve and
sixteen inches high and made of some dark brown wood.
Though very primitive, they were pretty and evidence of
unusual artistic ability. Mahine saw how interested the
Europeans were and rushed off inland intent on getting hold
of more of them. When he returned with a whole armful,
Forster saw that the motifs were repeated again and again,
one being copied from the other. Among them, however, was
one that was truly sensational. This was quite different from
the others in every way: it was life size and made of a light-
yellow wood and depicted a woman's hand. The fingers,
beautifully carved, were those of a dancer and ended in long,
well-tended nails. Nowhere on the island was there any timber
of the kind used for this carving, nor any sign that the women
of Easter Island tended their nails as the carving indicated.
Seeing how interested Forster was, Mahine, who had become
very fond of him during the voyage, made him a present of the
hand, and when they returned to England Forster presented it
to the British Museum where it still is.

In contrast to earlier occasions, the islanders did not turn
out in crowds to meet the English. Cook who, going by the
descriptions of the Dutch and Spaniards, had been expecting
to find a race of giants, encountered only people of small
stature, slight and looking rather wan and wretched. This and
other factors inclined Cook to believe that the island must
have been ravaged by some cataclysm or epidemic after the
Spaniards had been there and that this had decimated the
population. Later, remembering that they had seen no women
or children, it occurred to him that perhaps the inhabitants
had hidden in the underground hide-outs that the Spaniards
had mentioned. The patrols sent out by Cook observed at
many points of the island stone mounds with narrow openings
looking like entrances to subterranean caverns. The islanders
had not allowed the patrols to approach the mounds, so that
they had not been able to examine them. Exhausted by scurvy
and antarctic sailing and not wishing to risk a brush with the
islanders, they abandoned all further attempts to solve this
particular mystery.

The British rested at Easter Island for two weeks, then
Cook decided to sail on. Before this, however, he ordered that

supplies of fresh food should be bought. Once again he found that the inhabitants were only too eager to barter, but had no desire to give things for nothing. As fresh meat they offered chickens and rats; as vegetables, potatoes and sugar cane. Even here the English were cheated, for the cunning islanders gave them the baskets filled with stones topped with a thin layer of potatoes.

On 16th March 1774 the two English ships set sail, and so ended the third European visit to Easter Island.

Stone statues photographed on the slopes of the volcano Rano Raraku

(*above left*) Easter Island woman drawn by Hodges of the Cook expedition in 1774; (*above right*) Estevan—an Easter Island man, drawn by Miklucho-Maklaj; (*below*) man and woman of Easter Island, drawn by Radiguet of the French expedition led by A. Dupetit-Thouars

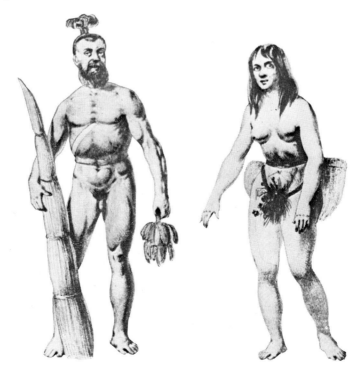

V

FRENCH GENTLEMEN
AND POLYNESIAN BEAUTIES

La Pérouse stood on deck watching the slowly sinking horizon that was the rocky coast of Brittany. For twenty years he had been sailing the seas for the honour of France, mostly on errands of war. This, his nineteenth voyage, was for a peaceful purpose and yet it promised to be no less dangerous than the others. Its purpose was that of almost all the important expeditions of the eighteenth century: to find the Terra Incognita of the south hemisphere. France, not wishing to be outdistanced in the international race to the Far South, especially by England, had been sending out one expedition after the other with this sole aim, though so far without success. The only result of the expeditions of Bouvet (1739), Bougainville (1766), Kerguelen (1771) and Marion and Crozet (1772) had been the discovery in the southern stretches of the Atlantic, Pacific and Indian Oceans, of some tiny, mostly uninhabited islands. Now another such expedition had been despatched under the command of Captain Jean Francois de Galaup, Count of La Pérouse. The Count was not an explorer like Columbus or Vasco da Gama, nor a traveller of the style of Captain Cook; he was first and last a sailor, a lover of the sea who had brought the mariner's art to perfection. Persistence and conscientiousness in fulfilling the tasks laid upon him were his main features. He was courageous, but not foolhardy, careful of the lives of the crews under him and of the soundness of his ships. Though he had sailed much in little frequented waters, he had never ventured into seas that were absolutely unknown. He was a brave soldier and mariner and at the same time a typical French gentleman of the Age of Enlightenment, an ardent supporter and pupil of Jean Jacques Rousseau. His way of thinking was more that of the scholar and philosopher than of the regular officer. Thus there was nothing surprising in his being given command of this new expedition with its two ships *Boussole* and *Astrolabe*.

The members of the expedition included specialists in

various branches of science: mathematics and astronomy,
natural science and meteorology, physics and geology, as well
as a physician and a botanist. They even had one of the royal
gardeners with them. He was to make plantations of
European vegetables and fruits in the newly discovered lands
and so had taken with him a considerable quantity of seeds
and also domestic animals, hoping to be able to teach the
natives of the new lands how to breed them. There was, too, a
painter whose duties were those of a modern photographer, to
record on paper the aspect of the lands they visited, the people
and scenes they saw. Thus well-equipped, the expedition had
left Brest on 1st August 1785 and headed south-west, making
for the coast of South America.

No sooner had the land of France disappeared below the
horizon than La Pérouse handed over to Captain Langle and
went below to his cabin once more to study his instructions,
especially those relating to the search of the southern Pacific,
of which he entertained high hopes. There he could read that
on 16th November 1770 the Spaniards had landed on Easter
Island and named it San Carlos and among the maps he had
been given was a copy of that of the island made by the
Spaniards who had actually sailed round it. The more he
studied the latter, the more intrigued and interested he
became.

The expedition rounded the Horn in January 1786 and
sailed out into the Pacific. After spending several weeks on the
Chilean coast the expedition set sail again in the middle of
March, heading west. When only a short way out from land
the water round the two ships began to boil as a school of
whales swam round them, coming so close as to shower the
decks with water when they blew.

They passed the island of Juan Fernandez without seeing it
as they made straight for Easter Island. According to La
Pérouse's calculation they should have been no more than
sixty miles from the island on 4th April, yet on that day they
had still seen none of the sea birds that other expeditions had
encountered in that part of the ocean. This was disquieting
enough, but worse was the fact that another four days passed
without any sign of the island. What could have happened to
it? Had the ocean swallowed it up? Was the map inaccurate?
Or had they gone wrong in their reckoning?

Then, about two o'clock on the afternoon of 8th April land
suddenly appeared on the horizon. There was no doubt: it was
Easter Island.

Taking advantage of a fine bright night the French ships sailed along the coast at a distance of about three miles and about eleven o'clock on the morning of 9th April they cast anchor in the same bay as Captain Cook.

As with previous visitors the islanders flocked out to meet the French ships and thronged the decks. They were unarmed and behaved in a very friendly manner. Wishing to win them over thoroughly before going ashore, La Pérouse ordered the distribution of trifling little presents brought with them for the purpose. Great success was enjoyed by small half-yard lengths of coloured linen, which the islanders seem to prefer to metal objects such as nails, knives or even scissors; but the thing they desired most was hats and of these the French had brought far too few to be able to satisfy everyone. Towards evening the exhausted Frenchmen began gesturing to give their guests to understand that it was time to leave. Reluctantly, though obediently, they dropped into the water and swam to shore carefully holding their presents in a bundle high above their heads.

Early the next morning La Pérouse gave orders to start landing. About sixty, including officers and the scientists, were to go ashore, leaving only skeleton crews aboard. Despite the friendly attitude of the islanders, the cautious La Pérouse ordered them to take with them four small cannon and twelve armed sailors. They all landed without hindrance and it was not long before the French found themselves gathered on the beach near the huge stone statue known from Captain Cook's account of the island, round which were gathered to meet them some five hundred islanders, all unarmed and mostly naked. Some were wearing pieces of yellow linen and all were tattooed and beaming in childish delight at their visitors.

The first thing the French did was to pitch a large tent in the middle of the small vacant space and in this they put the supplies and presents they had brought from the ships and posted armed guards to prevent them being stolen, the islanders now being notorious for their thieving propensities. But the guards were of little use. The cunning islanders, as though sensing that their new visitors were very susceptible to female charms, employed against them their most effective weapon — their women.

These were present in numbers such as no other expedition had seen. It looked as though half the throng were women and the place swarmed with children of all ages, which, again, previous visitors had scarcely seen. The women of Easter

Island, as the French were not slow to note, were unusually good-looking even for Oceania. They were well built, had regular features and pleasing golden-bronze-coloured skins. Without losing any time the women of Easter Island got down to business, offering their favours in a way about which the amazed Frenchmen could have no doubts. If they had, these were at once dispelled by the men of the island who made it abundantly clear that they not only had no objection to their visitors enjoying the favours of their wives and daughters, but even encouraged it, thrusting them into each other's arms. The French did not need asking twice. They found it easy to understand the lovely Easter Islanders and before they knew it their first morning in paradise had sped. It was only when orders were given for them to get ready to march off that they realized into what sort of a trap they had fallen. Almost everyone had had his pockets emptied and many of them discovered that various essential articles of their attire were missing. Afraid of possible squabbles, La Pérouse ordered that no one was to try to recover his property, everyone being promised compensation for his losses.

La Pérouse had not intended to spend more than eight or ten hours on the island and so, wishing to see as much as possible, he divided his men into three groups: one, under Lieutenant d'Escuere, was to guard the tent and their supplies; the second, under Captain Langle, was to penetrate as far inland as it could in the time, make contact with the inhabitants, examine their agriculture and, if the examination of the soil promised success, the expedition's gardener, who was one of the group, was to sow some of his seeds (of oranges, lemons, Indian corn, cotton and grain). The group was also to present the islanders with breeding pairs of various domestic animals: goats, sheep and pigs in order to start them breeding them. Needless to say, the experiment failed before it began, for the hungry islanders ate everything before it had time to breed or multiply, so that the island retained its appearance and character unchanged.

The third group, with La Pérouse in command, was to remain in the vicinity of where they had landed, so as not to waste time on marching about, and study the local stone statues, the buildings and plantations as thoroughly as time allowed.

Like earlier visitors, the French got the impression that the islanders seemed to appear on the treeless, arid surface of their mysterious island out of the bowels of the earth. They found that this was in fact what happened: the islanders *did* crawl out from subterranean dwellings. The friendly islanders allowed the French as far as the narrow entrances to their underground dens, a thing they had denied the English. The investigations of La Pérouse and his men showed that Captain Cook had been right in supposing that the islanders were hiding from their strange visitors in underground caverns. When the previous expedition had landed the island's elite as well as the women and children had hidden from them, and La Pérouse attributed the fact that they had plucked up courage to crowd round the French and even allow their women and children to mingle with them, to the good, friendly behaviour of Cook and his men.

La Pérouse's examination of the mysterious stone statues and the discovery in them of large quantities of human bones showed that they were tombs and very old.

> The largest that we looked at [wrote La Pérouse] was whitened with water and lime. Other mausoleums made of heaped stones are to be found beside the shore and hidden in them are tombs. One of the islanders gave clear indication of this, stretching out full length on the ground, then raising his hands to heaven telling us without any doubt that the islanders believe in life beyond the grave. I was far from supposing this and refused to accept the hypothesis, yet when he repeated the gestures again and again and Captain Langle on his return from the interior, told us a similar story, my doubts were dispelled. I believe even that all our Officers and passengers share this opinion. Yet we never came across traces of any cult and I do not think that anyone could suppose the statues to be idols, although the islanders do show them respect. These busts of enormous proportions are evidence that the islanders have not made much progress in the art of sculpture. They are made of rock of volcanic origin which scientists call *lapillo*.*

The French were particularly interested in the level of agriculture in the island. They found that only about one-tenth of the area was cultivated and they reckoned that three days' work in the fields annually was all each islander needed to do in order to obtain food for the year. Even so the fields and plantations were cultivated with great care: they were weeded, watered and fertilized with the ash of burned stalks. The bananas grew in regular lines.

---

* *Voyage de la Perouse autour du Monde, 1797*

It appeared that the islanders lived in communal societies to which the tilled land belonged and which were headed by local leaders or heads of families. The French were not able to establish this for certain, but they were given the impression that the islanders' unit was not the family, the women and children being in a way common property, that of the community in question.

As for dwellings, the French saw houses built of stones as well as subterranean caverns.

La Pérouse returned to the tent at one o'clock in the afternoon intending to allow his second-in-command, Clouard, who had remained aboard ship, to have a turn ashore. He found the men left to watch the tent in a lamentable condition. One and all were without hat, neckcloth and various other garments. In this they were not alone. Even their commander had been a victim of the islanders' sleight-of-hand, for when one of them obligingly helped him down from a tall rock pedestal, as he let go of him he whipped the hat off his head and disappeared. La Pérouse had no intention of pursuing any islander, so he let him go. When, on his return, he looked round, he had to laugh: not one of his group was left with a hat, to say nothing of other no less important articles of dress.

Although the French took the islanders' thieving with good humour it ceased to be a joke when two officers from *Astrolabe* reported that islanders had cut the sloop's moorings and stolen an anchor from the ship. As it was essential to have the anchor if they were to continue the voyage, La Pérouse ordered the thieves to be pursued into the interior. The two officers and their men who were given the task of recovering the anchor were pelted with stones. They fired a volley or two into the air and when this produced no effect, turned their muskets on the islanders, probably wounding several. They did not manage to get hold of the thieves, however; they no doubt being safe and sound in some subterranean cavern.

Even though there had been this nasty incident, the islanders remained incredibly kind and friendly and, when the soldiers went back to the tent, hurried after them and pressed their women folk upon them as if nothing had happened. About the same time Captain Langle returned from the interior with his detachment. Exhausted with the heat and his long march, he sat on a large stone in the shade of the tent and reported to La Pérouse.

We set out at 8 a.m. In the interior we came across large plantations of yams and sweet potatoes. The soil there was fertile and our botanist considered it suitable for planting the seeds we brought with us, so he sowed cabbage, beet and maize. Using sign language we explained that the seeds would produce edible roots and fruit. The islanders listened to the botanist's explanations with great interest and seemed to understand and then showed us places of even better land. There we sowed cotton and citrus fruits and tried to explain that the seed would grow into bushes and trees.

Later on we came across different kinds of stone dwellings, but mostly just long platforms. Through openings in the stones we saw skeletons inside and it seems that the islanders use these openings to communicate with their dead. One of the islanders graphically explained how the dead went to heaven. Further on, by the sea, we found stone pyramids built of stones piled up like the piles of cannon balls you see in artillery parks. Nearby were numbers of human bones and statues. All the statues were turned with their backs to the sea. Beside them we found models of people some ten or twelve feet high. I imagine that these were perhaps models for the sculptors of the stone statues. Further again, not far from the statues, a platform had been built of stones. This was 130 metres long and we could not make out what it was for. Perhaps it was a water cistern — perhaps an unfinished stone fortification.

At the most southerly point of the island, we found the crater of a volcano which we presumed extinct. Its size and the regularity of the shorn off sides are wonderful. The ground at the base of the volcano is boggy and overgrown with lush grass showing that it is fertile. That, too, was the only place in the island that we saw birds — they were terns.

Before coming back we presented the islanders with the domestic animals we had brought. The islanders promised to look after them and let them breed. The islanders we came across were peaceable and very hospitable. The regaled us with sweet potato and sugar cane. They did not however neglect any opportunity to steal. Nowhere did we see anyone who might have been older then sixty.

La Pérouse now gave orders to prepare to re-embark and at ten o'clock that same evening the two ships set sail and left Cook's bay and the hospitable island, heading north in bright moonlight.

For two more years La Pérouse sailed the Pacific until in 1788 Fate caught up with him on the coast of the island of Vanikora where he died in mysterious circumstances.

The thieving instincts of the Easter Islanders and his dealing with the inhabitants of the other exotic places he visited seriously undermined La Pérouse's faith in the teaching of his master, Rousseau, and in his concept of the "noble savage" and caused him to write this in his diary: "The philosophers write their works at their own firesides, while I have been travelling for thirty years. I have witnessed the injustice and deceit of the peoples who are considered good just because they live in the lap of Nature. However, Nature is straight in the mass only, but neglects all the details . . . Natural man is barbarous, evil and dishonest."

The next French ship to visit the island was *Venus* in 1830. The ship was there so short a time that none of her company even went ashore. Nonetheless they made contact with the islanders who, as always, came out and swarmed up on deck. Comparing their behaviour with the reports of previous visitors, the French noticed a certain rationalization at least among some of them — for example, one of the girls had brought with her a large basket, evidently hoping to collect lots of presents from the sailors. This did not surprise the French, who knew of the events during Moerenhout's recent visit to the island. The Frenchman had put in there on his way from Chile to Tahiti. Almost as soon as they arrived an islander had appeared on deck and made a completely unambiguous offer, inviting the visitors to go ashore and amuse themselves with the island's girls. Evidently the islanders were well aware what appealed to the tastes and interest of their visitors and cutely drew every advantage from it.

During the *Venus'* visit one of the island's girls visiting the ship had danced for the French an extravagant dance, a parody of the minuet. Most certainly the spectacle of her dance had nothing in common with the beauty of the culture and art of the Polynesian peoples. It obviously was stamped with the destructive influence of the visits of Europeans to the island, which were becoming more and more frequent and more harmful.

VI

RUSSIAN EXPLORERS

Even though Russian trade with Southern America and its own colonization there was expanding, the Russo-American Company, founded during the reign of the Empress Catherine II, was finding it more and more difficult to maintain contact with its factories in Alaska and the Pacific coast of America and to supply them. The route overland across the Urals and the whole Asiatic continent to the Sea of Ochotsk and thence across the Straits to Alaska was not only lengthy in time, but costly and unsafe. This led as early as the end of the eighteenth century to the concept of trying to link the Russian colonies in America with the homeland by the direct westerly sea route. The Napoleonic wars did not prevent the idea being tested out by the then Minister of Trade, Duke Rumancow, and the Minister of the Marine, Admiral Mordwinow, after receiving the approval of the Tsar Alexander I.

The plan was to send out an expedition from Kronstadt on the Baltic, across the Atlantic and down to Cape Horn and then up to Alaska. There the expedition would make for the coasts of China and Japan, as it had with it a Russian ambassador to the Emperor of Japan together with his suite. Having delivered the ambassador, the expedition was to return to Russia along the coasts of Asia and Africa, thus accomplishing the first circumnavigation of the world under the Russian flag.

The expedition was given two splendidly equipped ships *Nadiezda* and *Newa* and was put under an experienced sailor, Captain J.F. Kruzensztern. *Newa* was commanded by the expeditions's second-in-command, Captain Lisjanski. Bad weather prevented them leaving Kronstad until 7th August 1803, three weeks late. In March 1804 the two ships rounded the Horn and then sailed north-west. On 24th March, Captain Lisjanski lost sight of *Nadiezda* in thick fog and, unable to find her subsequently, headed for Easter Island, the *rendez-vous* agreed in the event of the two ships becoming separated.

The crew were considerably agitated by the loss of contact with the other ship in those little-visited waters of the vast ocean, where they were hundreds of miles from any settlement and forced to rely solely on themselves in any emergency. Their anxieties proved well founded, for on 28th March squalls blew up from the south-west, whipping up the waves and almost breaking *Newa's* fore-mast, which was only saved by the quick wit of some sailors who furled the sails in time. The stormy weather persisted for several days, but *Newa* came through it, though still without having seen a sign of *Nadiezda*.

In the first half of April the weather improved considerably with the result that the ship's motion became slight enough for Lisjanski to order the forge to be set up on deck, whereupon the smiths began making knives, nails, shears and other things of iron intended as gifts or to barter with the inhabitants of the South Pacific islands. They also began making the first preparations for landing: fastening the anchors onto their chains and preparing the boats. Then they saw the first seagull.

At eleven o'clock on 16th April, Easter Island was sighted on the horizon at a distance of some thirty miles. The weather being misty with a drizzle, Lisjanski decided to postpone landing until the following morning and remained for the night at a distance from the island's rocky coast. Early the next morning sail was hoisted and the ship sailed along the southern coast of the island intending to make a landing on the now traditional place — Cook Bay. As she sailed along *Newa* passed two dangerous rocks that pierced the surface off the south-west point looking deceptively like a ship with spread sails.

The scene that met their gaze on the south and eastern shores was particularly pleasing: fresh green grass studded with groups of banana trees. Those looking through spy-glasses could see in one place two huge stone statues standing on a common plinth. Further on, at the entrance to Cook Bay, they saw three more huge statues and beside them a fourth that was smaller and appeared to have been damaged. They looked exactly as La Perouse had described them.

The weather, however, had not improved sufficiently to allow them to put into Cook Bay; but Lisjanski decided to wait off-shore for some days for Kruzensztern in accordance with his instructions. On 18th April *Newa* sailed on northwards along the eastern side of the island. The shores here provided as pleasant a sight as those further south. As they sailed along close inshore they saw several scattered huts standing in thin groves of trees. People poured out of the huts and followed the ships along the coast in a throng. They saw five more groups of stone statues. The first group consisting of four statues appeared as soon as they had passed the southern point of the island. The second consisted of three statues. The third group was the same as that they had seen the previous day. The fourth and fifth stood at no great distance from the western headland and near them was a large number of buildings, while the land was more carefully tilled than in any other place on the island they had seen. They also observed numerous stone mounds, the tops of which were covered with something white, though they could not make out what it was.

A strong north-westerly was whipping up the waves and making it impossible to anchor. Not until nearly sunset did the wind slacken, but even so it drove the ships well north of the east cape. All the time the ship was sailing along the coast, it was accompanied by clouds of flying fish and flocks of sea-birds of various kinds.

Early the next morning sail was set once more and *Newa* continued along the north coast of the island. The wind was light, but the seas big. At first Lisjanski had ordered that *Newa* was to sail as close to the shore as possible, but frequent calms and showers of rain prevented this. Nonetheless, they tried to be no further than five miles out, so as to be able to observe the land through their glasses. Thus they were able to note that this part of the island was much more sparsely populated. Nonetheless they sighted four more stone monuments: the first consisting of only one statue, the second and third of two and the fourth of three statues. When the ship was close enough to be visible from shore, fires shone out from several places as the islanders signalled to their visitors. The Russians regarded these signals as an invitation and they would have liked to have taken advantage of it, only nowhere could they find a suitable landing place, even though they lowered a small boat and sent it to reconnoitre and take soundings off the shore.

Throughout 20th April the weather was so uncertain that they had to cease all observation of the northern coast of the island and return to the western side, where Lisjanski hoped to find better conditions for anchoring. However, from early morning on the 21st the weather was again so stormy that it took them until eight o'clock that evening to reach Cook Bay where they had intended to anchor and this was made impossible by a south-westerly gale.

Lisjanski was determined at all costs to leave some evidence of his visit, so that the *Nadiezda*, if she arrived, should know that those in *Newa* were alive and carrying out the plan, and might even be able to catch them up. He therefore ordered Lieutenant Paul Powaliszyn to take a small boat close in and present those who swam out to it with knives, pieces of iron, empty bottles and pieces of coloured cloth. At the same time Powaliszyn was to reconnoitre the bay as well as he could and take soundings, but not to attempt to land. At two o'clock that afternoon the boat returned to *Newa* laden with vegetables and fruits: bananas, sugar cane, yams and sweet potatoes.

Lieutenant Powaliszyn reported how, as soon as the boat had approached the shore, a group of men and women had emerged from the throng on the beach and with loud cries and signs of delight flung themselves into the water and began to swim out to it. As they swam they pointed to places suitable for landing. When they realized that the Russians were not intending to land, some thirty of them began swimming out to the boat despite the roughness of the sea. Seeing this, Lieutenant Powaliszyn had stood up and gesturing to them to come, had called out: "*Taio! Taio!*" the Tahitian for 'a friend'. To the first islander who reached the boat he gave the sealed bottle containing a letter for Captain Kruzensztern and in sign language tried to make him understand that he was to give the bottle to a ship like the *Newa* which was coming along behind her. Then, again in accordance with his instructions, he handed out knives, copper Russian coins strung on wire to make necklaces, some pieces of patterned material and some empty mustard jars fastened to pieces of wood on which *Newa's* name had been carved. What interested and delighted the islanders most were the knives they were given and the lieutenant regretted not having brought more. He had so few, in fact, that when the last to come, an elderly islander who appeared to be about sixty, reached the boat, they had nothing to give him but a coin-necklace and other trifles, but the old man was delighted, gave them a woven grass basket of sweet potatoes and everything he was wearing: including a small woven mat that he used to help him in swimming. Judging by this man's behaviour, it was not his first encounter with Europeans. He was the only one of those who swam out to have long hair and a thick reddish beard. The others were beardless and had short hair. They expressed a desire to go out to the ship, but were told in gesture that the distance was too great. Judging by the fact that the islanders aided themselves in swimming with bundles of reeds or wickerwork, Lieutenant Powaliszyn assumed that the boats previously observed by La Pérouse no longer existed. He estimated that there must have been five hundred people, including children, gathered on the shore, but confessed that they had been so occupied with the islanders in the water round the boat that they had not been able to devote much attention to the throng on the shore. Nor did any of them remember having seen a woman among them, though they had noticed figures dressed in short, fluttering garments. Many of the islanders had waved kerchiefs and pieces of clothing to them in a friendly way.

They judged that the islanders who had swum out to the boat were tall, about 1.80 metres. They had complexions like sunburned Europeans and the visitors who had read Forster's description of the long-eared islanders were expecting to find them all with long, pierced ears, yet of the scores they saw none had ears any different from their own.

The famous statues, judging by what the lieutenant had been able to see, were made of stone, about 13 feet high, about one-quarter of the total being accounted for by the cylindrical object on top of the head.

There was not much to say of the islanders' handiwork, but it pointed to their being good with their hands. The basket the older man had given to the lieutenant was some 16 inches by 10 inches, tightly and evenly woven of tough grass. The woven piece he used as a paddle was 1.35 metres long and the work in it in no way inferior to European workmanship.

The Russians then measured the length and breadth of the island and about six o'clock in the evening of 26th April 1804, taking advantage of a favourable wind, *Newa* sailed from the island, it having been decided to wait no longer for the other ships, heading for the Marquesas.

Meanwhile, after the ships had parted company in the fog, Kruzensztern had taken the surprising decision to sail straight to Kamchatka, where he intended to tranship the goods of the Russo-American Company; but, as he had been unable to inform Captain Lisjanski of the change of route, he decided to meet him at Easter Island some 500 miles away as had been agreed in the event of the ships becoming separated. As a result of unfavourable winds *Nadiezda* passed Easter Island at a considerable distance and did not meet up with *Newa* until 10th May 1804 off the island of Nukahiwa farther west.

The next Russian visit to Easter Island was in 1816, when *Ruryk* put in and some of her crew landed with unexpected results. As the first boat reached the beach, the throng of islanders that had assembled began trying to barter fruit and vegetables for nails. This was accompanied by much noise and confusion, of which more than one islander took advantage, purloining some trifle or other from the Russians. When the second boat reached the shore, the confusion became even worse. The islanders began shouting at each other, uttering inarticulate sounds. The laughing and shouting throng eventually quite blocked the one narrow beach on which you could land, forcing the Russians to push their boats back into the water. At that the delight of the islanders turned into hostility. An ugly murmur arose from the throng and from it stones began flying towards the retreating boats. Losing patience, the Russians fired a few shots in the air, at which the islanders scattered in all directions like a flock of sparrows. After that the Russians were able to land unhindered.

The Russians were not long free of the intrusive islanders who soon began noisily swarming round them again. When their attitude again became too aggressive, Kotzebue ordered a few more salvos to be fired into the air. After this, however, the islanders had grown accustomed to the sound of gunfire and became more importunate. Finally, Kotzebue, realizing that he was not going to reach the interior without using force, which he wished to avoid doing, decided to abandon the idea and ordered a return to the ship.

Among those who landed was Adelbert von Chamisso, a poet representative of German romanticism, but also a natural scientist. On his return he wrote a paper in which he imparted a lot of interesting things about the island which, he said, was a broad mountain crest, triangular in shape, at the corners of which tall pinnacles stood up like pyramids. From a distance the island appeared to be volcanic, rocky, covered with low grass and almost without sweet water or trees. He recorded several huge stone statues on the southeast coast of the island, but those Lisjanski had recorded at Cook Bay seemed to have vanished.

According to Chamisso the islanders were good-looking, well built and had nice expressions. He came to the conclusion that the swarthy, sprightly appearance of the old people they had encountered was due to a lack of disease in the island. Many of the islanders, he wrote, were tattooed. The blueish lines of the tattooing on their bodies consisted of streaks skilfully following the direction of the muscles and standing out distinctly against the swarthy background of their skins. Many of those who came to greet the Russian ship were dressed in white and yellow coats of a woven material made of bast. In their hair, which some of them wore cut short, others, long, they had garlands of leaves. Some of the islanders wore headdresses of black feathers. Many wore necklaces ornamented in front with a polished shell ground into the shape of a disk.

Chamisso was struck by the absence of ugly deliberate misshaping of the lips or nose seen among so many exotic peoples. All he saw was a few old men with greatly enlarged lobes to their ears. These were rolled up and inserted into a hole made in the top of the lobe with the result that these were not in any way off-putting, so Chamisso said. Some of the islanders had had their front teeth knocked out.

Chamisso noticed a fairly small group of young people whose skins were very much lighter than most of the others'. In the throng he noticed only a few women. Their faces were rouged which gave them an unpleasant look. They were not distinguished by their looks nor did the men seem to hold them in any esteem.

The Russians, of course, could not understand why the islanders appeared afraid of the ship and her boats, nor why they should be hostile. It was only later in the Hawaian islands that Kotzebue learned the truth of the matter from Alexander Adams, captain of an American brig. Adams told him that in 1807 he had been hunting seals off Mas-a-fuera, a small island to the west of Juan Fernandez to which Chile sent her convicts. Adams, however, was so short of men that he was unable to hunt, every member of the crew having to be continually on deck helping sail the brig which had to remain under sail in order not to fall prey to the current there. Adams, therefore, decided to go to Easter Island for the hands he needed.

He anchored his brig, *Nancy*, in Cook Bay and after a bloody battle with the islanders, managed to seize twelve men and ten women, whom they put in chains and locked up. After three days' sailing, when they judged the brig was far enough from the island, they brought their prisoners up on deck and removed their chains. The moment they were freed, the Easter Islanders rushed to the rail and jumped overboard. The Americans just managed to restrain the women by force from doing the same. Adams gave orders to heave-to and let the ship drift, reckoning that the islanders would tire and come back to the ship on their own. They waited for them to do so; but they soon saw that the Easter Islanders, accustomed since childhood to swimming and not realizing the distance between them and home, were going to try to swim back — or else they preferred certain death to slavery.

After a brief discussion among themselves the islanders had divided into two groups, one swimming off in the direction of Easter Island, the other heading north. This irritated Adams and he sent his boats after them. But all the Americans' attempts to fish the islanders out of the water were in vain. Each time a boat approached one of them, he dived and escaped. In the end, the Americans gave up and returned to the *Nancy*, leaving the islanders to their fate. Thus it was only the women Adams brought to Mas-a-fuera. Subsequently Adams made other raids on Easter Island kidnapping more of its inhabitants.

VII

THE ENGLISH RETURN

One of the main and most intriguing objectives of the polar expeditions of the first half of the nineteenth century was the search for the North-West Passage, the sea route along the icebound north coast of the American continent from the Atlantic to the Pacific. In those days, before anyone had thought of building the Panama Canal, to get from the Atlantic to the Pacific, you had to sail round South America, either through the treacherous Magellan Straits or round Cape Horn; thus the discovery of a north-west passage would have been an epoch-making event for sail. It was, then, not surprising that the maritime powers spent lavishly, sending out expedition after expedition in search of the Passage.

Here the English were the most energetic, for to them discovery of such a new route would have had the added importance of helping them defend their possessions in Canada which were then being seriously threatened by the Russian colonization of neighbouring Alaska, whence the Russians were already pushing southwards as far as distant California, founding numerous factories and laying the foundations of a Russian America.

Two of the largest expeditions sent from Britain in the 1820s were those commanded by Captain Parry and Captain John Franklin, which were planned on a huge scale. Assuming that if they got through the North-West Passage they would reach their objective, the Bering Straits, exhausted by the hardships of polar navigation, it was decided to send a supply ship to wait for them at the Bering Straits and afford whatever assistance they required. The ship chosen was *Blossom* under command of Captain Frederick William Beechey.

In those days to get from England to the Bering Straits meant sailing the whole of the Atlantic from north-east to south-west and then the whole length of the Pacific from south to north. On 19th May 1825, *Blossom* sailed from Spithead and after rounding the Horn reached Valparaiso in Chile in October of that year.

Leaving Valparaiso Beechey sailed west, intending to pass Juan Fernandez and so get its geographical position accurately fixed. Adverse winds, however, made him abandon the project and he passed the island at a considerable distance sailing straight to Sala-y-Gomez, in the region of which he encountered calms, as a result of which the ship made very slow progress, all the slower because each night as soon as darkness fell, they furled sail and hove-to until daybreak. This cautious procedure was dictated by two considerations: not to run onto one of the submerged reefs in which the waters round the island abound and not to miss the tiny scrap of land which is all the island is, by sailing past it in the dark.

On 14th November appeared the first birds they had seen since leaving Chile and the next morning they saw on the horizon three small crags: the island of Sala-y-Gomez. The ship's company found the island a most depressing sight: although they had been told that it was inhospitable, what they saw was even worse than they had expected. In front of them was a low lump of completely bare rock without any growth except a few miserable clumps of seaweed. The only living creatures they saw on the island were sea birds. Through their telescopes they could see planks and logs on the shore, presumably the remains of some wrecked ship. Having fixed its position and made various minor adjustments to the map drawn by previous expeditions, the British were glad to leave and continue westwards.

In the early afternoon of 16th November 1825 the look-out in the foremast sighted land on the horizon. This was Easter Island, the next call according to the expedition's plan. Sailing closer, Beechey decided to anchor for the night and sail along the northern side of the island in the morning, following the route taken by Captain Cook half a century before.

As they sailed along the English scrutinized the island's settlements upon the cliffs, especially the long houses built in the shade of banana trees. Familiar with the accounts of Cook, La Perouse and Kotzebue, they kept a sharp look-out for the mysterious statues and it was not long before they saw the huge bulk of one of the *moai* from which rose four great statues exactly like those described by La Perouse.

The British differed from the earlier visitors in praising the level of the island's agriculture, describing their system of irrigating their fields with water from a lake in the crater of an extinct volcano, a thing none of the others had even observed. The British again were the only ones to mention seeing groves of trees and bushes on the island.

As the ship sailed slowly along, an ever-growing crowd of islanders kept pace with it on shore. Every now and again the throng would halt, light a bonfire and signal to the sailors. When the ship reached the north-west headland, the captain ordered that she should be hove-to and a boat lowered to take soundings. The moment the islanders saw this being done, they thronged to the beach expecting the boat to land. The sea at this point bristled with treacherous and submerged reefs on any one of which the boat might have been stove-in. Some of the islanders removed parts of their clothing and waved them to warn the sailors; others impatiently jumping into the water swam out to meet the boat and before long it was surrounded by bobbing heads and friendly waving hands. The attitude of the islanders was astoundingly friendly. It was as if they had already forgotten the recent nasty incident when the captain of an American ship had forcibly carried off a dozen or more of their numbers intending to colonize Mas-a-fuera. The British who knew of the incident, had anticipated being given if anything a hostile reception and the contrary was a pleasant surprise.

Having finished sounding, the ship sailed on during the afternoon, continuing along the western coast of the island until she reached the bay where previously Cook and La Perouse had anchored. The islanders had followed all the way on shore, lighting fires to indicate the way. The largest of these fires was lit at the bay where landing was possible and there a great throng assembled.

Beechey decided to go ashore, but to be on the safe side he first sent off two boatloads of well-armed sailors under Lieutenants Peard and Wainwright and with a few extra officers as well, even though he did not expect any hostile reaction at the first encounter. The expedition's naturalist also went with the first two boats. While the boats made for the bay, the ship remained well offshore. As the boats drew nearer, those in them were able to distinguish individuals in the throng; some were running up and down signalling to their visitors, while a few were throwing big stones down off a sort of rampart erected near the beach.

The closer the boats came, the greater the commotion on shore, until the noise was such that the sailors could scarcely hear the orders of their officers. Then almost to a man the throng of islanders dived into the water and swam out to the boats, round which the water boiled, so that the sailors had to

stop rowing. Everywhere were raised arms and hands
grasping bananas, sugar cane, sweet potatoes, little carved
figures, nets and other things. Seeing that the newcomers did
not seem to want to barter, the islanders began throwing their
wares into the boats and using the hand thus freed to hang on
to gunwhale, stern or bows. The weight of those hanging on to
them pulled the boats down dangerously low in the water and
the sailors had no other course than to use their oars to push
the islanders away. The islanders, however, were not in any
way put out and did not even swim away, but remained in the
water waiting for their rewards. When these were not
forthcoming, they set about taking them, snatching various
trifles from the sailors.

Among the swimmers the sailors noticed quite a number of
young and even lovely women. The women were just as free-
and-easy as the men, snatching whatever they could or
helping the men by using their charms to distract the sailors'
attention. The islanders were so clever and skilful in
purloining that the British were all but as naked as the
islanders when they eventually stepped ashore, by which time
several islanders were dressed as British sailors.

Near the boats was a small rock jutting a few feet out of
the water and onto this swarmed many of the women to get a
breather after their long swim, so that the rock was covered
with wriggling wet bodies. As the boats passed close to the
rock, three or four of the women jumped back into the water
and swam towards the boats to try their luck with the visitors
from far away. One swam out hanging onto the shoulders of
an older man, seemingly her father, who appeared to offer her
to the sailors. She was young and very pretty and the men
were only too glad to take hold of her arms and haul her
aboard, where they sat her down among them. She was pretty
and shapely; she had small breasts, dark eyes and black hair
that fell to her swarthy shoulders. There was an arch of
tattooing on her forehead above each eyebrow. On the rest of
her body long narrow strips of blue tattooing ran down her
thighs to her knees. It was the same with the other women and
at a distance this made them look as if they were wearing
close-fitting knee-breeches. The girl's only garment was a big
triangle of woven grass strung from her hips. She appeared
quite at ease among the sailors and obviously had the same
ideas about property as had the other islanders, for she tried
to divest one of the officers of parts of his uniform. When she
failed in this, she began singing melodiously. Then, to the

horror of those in the boat, she began summoning the other women and when some swam out she seized them not too delicately by the hair and tried to haul them aboard; the officers had to order a stop. As the boat passed the rock, all the women on it joined in the girl's song and made friendly gestures to the sailors.

Just before the boats reached the shore, there was another rush towards them of islanders laden with island produce. The beach was so crowded that landing was impossible and the boats had to turn north. There with the help of the islanders who guided them through a labyrinth of submerged rocks, they found a suitable place and got ashore. The British decided that it was an expensive landing, for the islanders helped them with one hand and with the other deftly emptied their pockets. There was, of course, no question of recovering anything taken in this way, if only because to have tried to pursue one of those pickpockets through the throng would only have led to the loss of all the owner's other possessions and probably of his clothes as well. The British, with the islanders still swarming round them and unable to keep their distance, did not know what attitude to adopt: whether like Cook to punish any theft discovered and proved (and how?) or like La Pérouse to shut their eyes to it all.

As the British were getting out of the boats, two men stepped forward from out the throng. They wore headdresses of plumes, apparently pelican feathers, and appeared to be chiefs for the crowd obeyed them. It was only thanks to them ordering the throng to move back and make a narrow gangway that the British were able to get ashore at all. The islanders assumed that the first sailor to step ashore was the visitors' leader and they ceremoniously conducted him to the stone rampart and seated him on a block of lava, round which the throng of islanders stood in a semicircle. The next moment other islanders appeared with baskets of produce and insisted on bartering. On this occasion, however, they would not accept just anything. The British were not prepared for bartering and when one of them, with nothing else to offer, proferred a large ship's nail, it was angrily thrown aside and the profferer informed by signs that it was fish hooks the other required. Seeing that their visitors showed no eagerness to barter, the islanders began pressing and insisting that they did so, even to the extent of threatening. At last the sailors began to notice people with stout cudgels which they brandished threateningly. This the British took as a signal that it was time to withdraw. This, however, was not so easily done.

Meanwhile Beechey and the other officers on board were watching through field-glasses with growing concern. Their fears for the lives of the shore-party grew when they noticed a tall man of martial appearance all decked out in feathers emerge from one of the long narrow houses like boats turned bottom up, and behind him a group of men armed with short, stout cudgels, who headed straight for the landing-place. A moment later, they heard the ominous sound of trumpets, like the war trumpets the Polynesians made of large shells.

Lieutenant Peard had already given this tall leader a keepsake with which he at first seemed perfectly satisfied, but the insatiable islanders grew more and more insistent and so the British, having nothing else to offer them, began moving towards the boats in order to obtain further supplies. The islanders took the move as a retreat and began showing their displeasure in earnest, even holding the sailors back by force. The confusion increased when one of the sailors began struggling with an islander in an attempt to recover something the other had taken. The other islanders took advantage of the confusion to steal even more and the poor sailors, not knowing what to do, withdrew to their boat as fast as they could. This was the signal for the islanders to take the offensive. The attack was begun by the tall leader who hurled a large stone at Lieutenant Peard. The next moment the sailors were being bombarded with stones. Seeing what was happening, the islanders in the water round the boat hurried to the shore where they sought the shelter of the stone rampart, where they presumably felt safe from the Europeans' guns. It was obvious from their behaviour that this precaution was a lesson learned from earlier encounters with white visitors.

The strength of the bombardment increased and practically everyone in the boats had been hit by one or more of these stones which weighed a pound or so and were thrown with astounding accuracy. The only person who had not been hit was the girl sitting on the gunwhale who watched it all with absolute indifference as if it was no concern of hers. Lieutenant Wainwright first chivalrously tried to shield her, but then her attitude made him lose patience and he pushed her into the water.

Growing impatient, the British fired some shots into the air, but this had the contrary effect to that intended, for it angered the islanders who attacked with redoubled energy. The British then fired into the throng. The first and only victim of this salvo was the martial leader, who was probably killed. The British were now able to reach their boats without loss or other damage than bumps and bruises and they hurriedly left the island after a stay of only a few hours.

This British visit to Easter Island ends the era of true voyages of discovery. In the first half of the nineteenth century visits by ships with more or less hostile intentions towards the islanders became increasingly common. Acts of violence and killing became more and more frequent, leading up to the day when the wretched islanders would be all but exterminated.

VIII

THE END OF ITS GREATNESS

Not a breath of wind ruffled the perfectly smooth surface of the ocean. Although it was still early and the sun newly risen, the heat was intense beneath the cloudless sky. At a slight distance from the coast of the island of Te-pito-te-henua was a small craft made of woven reeds in which sat two swarthy islanders. The one, a youth, was energetically plying a short paddle of closely-woven grass as he drove his craft southwards. In the bows, legs tucked under him, sat an older man, his curly hair well speckled with white. In his lap lay dismantled fishing rods, tiny hooks and other fishing gear and he was so busy unravelling some lines, that he paid no attention to his surroundings.

The two came from the village of Anakena. The older man was called Rahi (meaning 'bright') and the younger, his son, Manu (bird) and they were taking advantage of the calm conditions to fish in the treacherous waters of the south-west coast of the island where fish abounded. Soon they rounded a headland and had the jagged silhouette of the inshore rocks and islets in view: Motu Nui, Motu Iti and Motu Hao Hao (meaning 'collection of rocks'). The water here was seething with eddies and swirls: Manu skilfully streered his craft among the rocks and reefs, even though an occasional wave struck the side and gave them an icy shower. Finally they reached the rock for which they were heading, landed and pulled the boat up behind them. They at once set about preparing their nets and rods. Having put them out, they sat down in the shade of a boulder. There was nothing to break the silence but the occasional slap of a wave on the rock or the strident cry of a circling seabird. The two worked in silence, keeping an eye on the birds to see they did not steal their catch.

About noon they refreshed themselves with a bathe, then took from the boat the food they had brought with them a few bananas, a little dried fish. The sun was almost at its zenith and to find shade they had to climb to a cave they knew of from previous visits. It was deliciously cool inside the cave and they stretched out to rest after their labours. As they lay there blissfully Rahi told his son the old island legend of how the Easter Islanders first obtained their bone fish hooks. This was the story:

In the reign of Atua Vre Rangei, the seventeenth of our kings, the carvers of our stone statues were relieved of all other work with the result that the poor fishermen had to work extra to keep them as well. In those days the hooks the fishermen used were made of stone so hard that it sometimes took a whole month to make one. Nevertheless even the best hook of the most skilful fishermen gave only a poor result. At that time there lived in the village of Anga Piko a youth called Ure Vaiu, who came from an ancient fisher family, one of the most skilful in the island. Although he had a number of stone hooks inherited from his ancestors, his own catches were poor, so poor that he was discouraged and often complained of his lot and his poverty.

Once, after a whole day of fruitless fishing, Ure Vaiu spent the night praying to Mea Kahi patron of fishers. As he prayed, there appeared to him the spirit of an old fisherman called Tira Kora, who told him that the sole cause of his lack of success was bad hooks. He advised him to go to the grotto where his father's remains were buried, dig up his bones and try to make hooks from them. Ure Vaiu was so terrified by the appearance of the ghost that at first he could not recall the advice given to him. But finally he did and went to the cave for his father's bones. For the next several days he went to sea in his boat and sat for hours wondering how to make hooks out of bone. Because he spent his time thinking instead of fishing and returned each evening with an empty boat, the others turned against him and began to taunt him over his incompetence. He paid no attention to their jeering and secretly worked away at making hooks of his father's bones. Finally, his hooks were made and he went well apart from the others to try them out.

The results exceeded all his hopes. From then on he returned home each evening with his boat laden with fish. His extraordinary success now aroused the envy of the others and as he steadfastly refused to tell them the secret of his success they began to hate him. One day, as Ure Vaiu was fishing as usual well apart from the others, he was attacked and made to pay for his secretiveness with his life. In the bottom of his boat were found his bone fish hooks and so the secret became common knowledge and ever since the fishermen of our island have had good catches.

As the sun was getting low, the two left the cave and set off homewards. They were in a hurry to get back as the next day was that appointed for the great annual ceremony of the Sacred Bird.

The following morning Manu and Rahi got up early and set off down the path that led to the volcano Rano Kao. There after a short wait, they saw a long procession with a trailing cloud of dust approaching from the village of Mataveri. These were pilgrims on their way to the sacred settlement of Orongo. For the last few weeks the pilgrims had been living apart in three long-houses on the fringe of Mataveri village, while they prepared themselves for the great occasion. Day after day they had practised the ceremonial dances and chants and devoted the rest of their time to making magnificent plumes, diadems and other ornaments. It was only now, the first day of July, that they had left their houses.

Almost all the inhabitants of the island were waiting to conduct those who were to take part in the noble competition for the highest honour it was possible for them to attain — the title of bird-man (*tangata manu*), which was accorded to the one who first found an egg of the *manu-tara* (bird-harbinger) or common tern (*sterna hirundo*) which nested on the cliffs of the south-west headland.

Having formed procession the pilgrims moved off towards the crater of Rano Kao on the steep slopes of which lay Orongo, from which one had a splendid view of the three rocky islets: Motu Nui, Motu Iti and Motu Hao Hao rising from the water like three needles.

As the procession drew nearer, the buzz of voices grew louder and the clouds of dust thicker. Rahi closely watched as the people passed, looking for Rue, his patron. The various leaders, *matato*, taking part in that year's competition, were each surrounded by a suite. Their faces were painted red and black making it difficult to discern their features. They wore magnificent feather headdresses and their hands held the ceremonial baton, *ao*. Leaping and jerking in time to the songs hummed by the crowd, they made their slow way up the steep side of the volcano following the path known since time immemmorial as 'the *ao* road'.

As they watched, Manu saw a broad-shouldered man striding at the head of a group of dancing figures. His skin was tattooed and now gaudily painted. On his head was a huge plume and in his hand an *ao* that he waved in time with the song. This was Rue. As the group came opposite them, Manu and Rahi joined the group of dancers and continued with them to the stone village of Orongo.

It was evening by the time they reached their destination. The rays of the setting sun turned the wrinkled sea golden. Here each *matato* with his suite took up quarters in one of the stone huts that lay scattered about the slopes of the crater. These huts stood empty throughout the year except for the short season of the ceremonies of the Sacred Bird. Rue removed his headdress and ornaments and rolled aside the boulder that blocked the entrance to the hut, then crawled inside through the narrow entrance. His suite followed, one by one. Manu, as one of the youngest, went in last.

Manu was visiting the sacred village for the first time so he was greatly interested in his surroundings. When his eyes had grown accustomed to the gloom inside, he saw that the stone walls were covered with lovely painted pictures, mostly of the God Make-Make and various forms of the Sacred Bird. Rue had seated himself on the ground in the middle of the floor with the older men gathered round him. In low voices they began discussing the morning's procedure and the best way of obtaining eggs of the *manu-tara*.

This was the first time young Manu had been admitted to the council of the elders and his heart was filled with delight and pride when he heard that Rue was entrusting him with the difficult but honourable function of being his *hopu*.* The hopu's job was far from easy. In the first place he had to swim the shark-infested strip of water separating Rano Kao from the islet Motu Nui and there climb up its steep sides and stay on the islet until he had found a *manu-tara* egg. If he succeeded he had to inform his patron on the island as swiftly as possible, hoping to get in ahead of the other *hopus* doing the same thing for their patrons.

Their deliberations finished, they all left the hut and set about lighting fires and preparing the evening meal. Manu was so excited and overcome by the honour that had been done him that he felt he must be alone for a while to think things over, and he walked away from the throng until he could no longer hear the buzz of voices. He sat himself on a boulder at the edge of the crater. Far below him boiled the sea, pounding and roaring at the foot of the volcano. The ever-turbulent waves kept changing colour: now white with foam, now sea-green, now dark blue; then the orange-coloured disc of the sun touched the horizon and cast streaks of golden-orange, red and green across it. Gradually Manu's bursting

*The word *hopu* has several meanings: snatcher, catcher, receiver, diver and to bathe.

pride gave way to apprehension at the thought of how the new day, or the following one at the latest, he would have to dive into those boiling waters and swim the treacherous, narrow channels. So deep in thought was he that he did not hear the footsteps behind him and only realized there was someone standing there when he felt a hand on his arm. He turned his head and smiled when he saw that it was Toorangi, who had been his friend and guardian ever since he could remember.

"Feeling afraid?" Toorangi asked.

Manu admitted that he was and the old man told him that he should have no fears, for many years before he himself had been *hopu* and not only survived but found the eggs of the *manu-tara* for his patron. Manu wanted him to tell him all about it, but the old man refused, saying that he had heard it all before; instead, he would tell him the legend of how the birds first came to the island.

Long, long ago, [the old man began] it is said there were no birds either on the big island or on Motu Nui. On Anga Nui was a stone on which lay a skull belonging to a witch called Hitu. One day a great wave washed the skull off the stone and into the sea. Seeing this the witch plunged into the boiling waters in an attempt to recover the skull. The skull was being swept farther and farther out and the old witch swam for many days in pursuit of it and finally she reached a small islet that rose steeply out of the water. The islet was quite white, being covered with a thick layer of guano from the birds that nested on it in great numbers. The waves cast the skull onto the islet and there it was at once transformed into Make-make, the ruler of Motu Torema Hiva (the native name for the island of Sala-y-Gomez).

The guardian of the sea-birds, Hana, kindly greeted the two visitors (Make and the witch) and they both stayed on the island to help Hana in his work. Make-make, however, had taken a liking to the island of Te-pito-te-henua and after a few days asked Hana to catch some birds which he could take with him to the island. Landing on Anga Nui he went thence to Poike and placed the birds among the rocks for them to nest there and then returned to his little island.

The following year he went back to see if the numbers of the birds had increased, but he was horrified to find that the inhabitants had taken the birds' eggs and eaten them. So he caught more birds and again put them among the rocks of Vaihu, but there the same thing happened as on Te-pito-te-henua, so he released the next lot of birds near Vai Atare. The inhabitants there were not so greedy and allowed the birds one egg each to sit on and thus were hatched the *manu-tara*. This satisfied Make-make who never went back to the island, but placed the next lot of birds he caught on *Montu Nui* and there they increased enormously and unto this very day the eggs of the *manu-tara* gathered in the spring on Moto Nui are a great delicacy and this, as you now know, we owe to the foresight of Make-make.

Darkness was already falling as Manu and Toorangi returned to Orongo. The sun had vanished and in its place a silvery full moon rode high in the grey-blue sky. With the disappearance of the sun came piercing cold and fires were flaring outside the stone huts lining the rim of the crater. Some of the people were still eating their evening meal, others were humming monotonous songs in praise of the Sacred Bird.

Rahi was already worried by his son's long absence and his first greeting was a reproach; but, when he saw that with him he had Toorangi, for whom he had great respect, he forgave him and inviting the two to take their seats at his fire, he hooked out from the ashes a few roast potatoes and a piece of chicken for them.

Rue, Rahi told them, was most impatient and wanted Manu to set off earlier than the other *hopu* and so he was to leave at dawn the next day. Having finished his supper, Manu crawled inside the hut and fell asleep in his place.

He slept like a log and Rahi had difficulty in shaking him awake at dawn. He had prepared a supply of food and this lay piled on a little raft of plaited rushes. So, after eating a little fruit, Manu and his father went to take leave of the *matato*.

They found Rue on his knees in the middle of the hut, surrounded by the elders murmuring the prayers: *Ka to'o ma Hana, ma Make-make*. The prayer finished, he made an offering of food to the God Make-make and his companion Hana. Then he prayed to Vie-kana, the bird-god who lives on Mataveri, ardently beseeching him to see that Manu should be the first to find the eggs. He knew perfectly well that if Make-make did not wish him to be man-bird that year, Rue's *hopu* would never see the eggs even if he trod on them. Having finished his prayers, Rue got to his feet and went to Manu to say goodbye and wish him good fortune.

Now came one of the most difficult parts of Manu's task. With his father helping him, he began lowering himself down the steep cliff face to the sea, the loaded raft strapped to his back. That done, Manu and Rahi made their way to the foot of the volcano where they sat on the narrow rocky foreshore to get their breath and for Manu to gather strength before tackling the swim across the strait which was not all that wide, but rough with swirls and eddies between submerged reefs and rocks that made it a dangerous undertaking.

Manu was impatient and wanted to start straight away so as to get it over and be on Motu Nui, but his father restrained him, appealing to his commonsense to rest properly. It was about noon when they embraced and Manu leaped lightly into the water. Rahi launched the little raft and Manu set off for Motu Nui, pushing ahead of him the raft on which was his bundle of food.

After a hard struggle of some quarter of an hour Manu reached the precipitous shore of Motu Nui and he had to swim about for quite a time before finding a place where he could land. This was not easy for the cliff rose almost vertically from the water and was impossible to climb, especially for someone with a load. Finally, Manu discovered a breach in the wall of rock and was able to climb it. For a long time he lay on the rock at the top gasping with the effort of the climb. He could not afford too long a rest, however, as before darkness fell he had to find some sort of shelter where he could cache his provisions which must last him for the next few days or even a week. So he climbed to the top, where without much difficulty he found a roomy, dry cave and there he stowed his provisions. The cave was full of signs of its having been used before: remains of food, bones, ashes from old fires and here and there on the walls were drawings mostly of the Sacred Bird. At the back of the cave Manu found an unfinished wooden figure started presumably by some *hopu* bored by the long wait for the manu-tara to lay its eggs.

So the days passed, one like the other. Other *hopus* made their appearance sent by their *matatos* on the same quest as Manu. When the weather was stormy, the boys were cut off from the main island and they had to economize with their provisions, even drying banana-skins and potato peel in the sun and putting it by as an iron ration. When the weather improved and the seas had subsided somewhat, people came across from the various *matatos* and the families of the *hopus* bringing them more provisions and news. Manu's father came once with a fresh supply of food and greetings from Rue.

The boys spent most of the day climbing the cliff and rocks in search of nests and jealously keeping any finds from each other. At odd moments they sat in the sun looking up into the sky at the circling black gulls, watching intently their every movement in the hope of discovering where they would choose to nest.

With the beginning of September the *hopus* on Motu Nui increased their vigilance. Scarcely giving themselves time to eat or sleep enough they seldom took their eyes off the gulls. One day, when all the other boys were busy watching the gulls circling overhead, Manu stole away and lowered himself onto a shelf of rock where he had for some time noticed that the gulls liked to sit. This time he was in luck, scarcely had his feet touched the short grass when he saw one of the spotted eggs of the *manu-tara*. Almost at a run he clambered up the rock known as Rangi-te-manu, and, cupping his hands round his mouth shouted as loudly as he could in the direction of the main island. "Rue shave your head!" The cry was heard on Orongo opposite where, during this time of waiting, people patrolled the headland known as Haka-rongo-manu (listener for the bird) day and night. At the news all the other *hopu* on Motu Nui were ordered to return to the main island in order to take part in the Sacred Bird ceremonies.

It was a proud and happy Manu who swam back across the strait with the precious egg securely fastened on his head. He had no fear now, for the first *manu-tara* egg has magic properties and could protect him from all harm. Nothing could happen to him.

Manu reached the shore and handed the egg to Rue, who lavished him with praises.

As soon as the name of the new man-bird was announced, Rue shaved his head, eyebrows and eyelashes. The priests placed a red scarf round his shoulders and presented the egg to him on a tray of sandalwood. During this solemn ceremony the choirs sang songs and hymns and the winner's family danced for joy. Then the new man-bird, his face painted with red and black stripes, a wooden bird fastened on his shoulders, placed himself at the head of the procession that was forming and they set off slowly downhill heading for Mataveri.

The real ceremony began first in Mataveri where in honour of the new man-bird the priests made human sacrifices to Make-make, the bodies being subsequently roasted on huge spits and eaten.* Manu was to remember the ceremonies, even though this was not the first time he had taken part in them. His delight was short-lived because on his return to his village, Anakena, he was met at the door of his home by his

---

*According to Alfred Metraux: *Easter Island*, New York 1957. Some authors doubt the accounts of cannibalism among the Easter Islanders.

Statue with its head-covering of volcanic tufa. Father Sebastien is in the front row, on the left

(*above*) An unfinished statue in the crater quarry on Rano Raraku; (*below*) *Hopu*, having found the egg of the *manu-tara*, presents it to his *matato*

mother who, with tears in her eyes, told him that his beloved 'grandfather' Toorangi had died that morning. He had fallen ill while Manu was on Motu Nui and though he had often said how much he wished to see Manu once more before he died, it had not been granted him.

The next day, the feast of the Sacred Bird being over, Manu's family, the closest kin of the dead man, began preparing Toorangi's funeral. When the day arrived, the body was wrapped in a woven tapa, wound round with cord and solemnly carried on a stretcher to the cemetery beside the ocean. There the stretcher was placed on the top of one of the stone *ahu* where it would remain for the next two or three years until either the sun had dried it like a mummy or the flesh had dropped off the bones leaving only a white skeleton. In either event the remains would be laid in the catacomb within the *ahu*.

Having placed Toorangi's body on the *ahu*, the procession now consisting of almost all the inhabitants of Anakena, went to a solemn repast given by Rahi. This lasted until late in the night and was accompanied by laments and ceremonial dances.

Such had been the life of the islanders for centuries almost without change, disturbed only by the more and more frequent visits of European ships. In the second half of the nineteenth century, however, a grave danger hung over the heads of the Easter Islanders. The 1860s saw a wave of slave-snatching in the Southern Pacific, when slavers forcibly abducted almost the entire population of many islands in Polynesia. One of the first to suffer this tragedy was the island closest to the American continent, Easter Island.

The immediate cause of the abduction was the expansion of the trade in guano. The Chinese immigrants not having fulfilled the expectation of those who brought them to Peru, it was decided to replace them with kanakas from the islands of Oceania.

On 12th December, 1862 a number of Peruvian slavers anchored in Hanga Roa bay. Some unsuspecting islanders who went aboard were at once put in irons and placed in the holds. When no others came to the ships and even the offer of presents failed to entice any more of the islanders on board, the slavers went ashore on a regular man-hunt, driving more than 1,000 or almost the whole of the then population aboard their ships. Among those captured in this way was the king of

Easter Island, Maurata, and his two sons, Tepito and Kerekorio, who spent the rest of their days digging guano on the island of Chincha.

This tragedy is really the epilogue to the age-long history of the Easter Islanders, for it destroyed their cultural and ethnographic individuality and made it impossible for later research to solve the mysteries of the Island.

IX

HOTUMATUA

The whole of Chincha stank with the sour smell of bird droppings. Within the first year more than half the thousand Easter Islanders had died and no wonder, for they were quite unaccustomed to hard work, had no resistance to disease and were quite unused to the heat. They died like flies, some of disease, some of homesickness. They lived almost in the open, with scarcely a roof over their heads and ate anything or nothing. They had little time to look after themselves, for the overseers kept them hard at it from morning until night loading into ships the stinking guano that made their eyes water and stung their throats and nostrils.

In the evenings king Maurata and his elder son, Tepito, would go among the people, trying to comfort them. Often the two would go and sit by the water's edge looking out in the direction of where Easter Island lay. Again and again Maurata made his son promise that if he himself did not return to Te-pito-te-henua, his son would lead the survivors back there as the great Hotumatua had done centuries before.

This legend of Hotumatua is one of the many that tell of the remote past of these strange people. According to it the home of the distant ancestors of the Easter Islanders was a large island far to the west of Easter Island. It was called Maraerenga and had a mild climate. On it were many trees of which the islanders built large boats and big houses. In spite of the shade, it did sometimes happen that people died of the heat.

The king of the island was Hotumatua and something happened that made him leave the land of his fathers. It is said that his brother, Te Ira-ka-tea, fell in love with the intended of another chief called Oroi. Pretending to be unable to make up her mind which of the two men she preferred, the girl told Oroi that she would marry him if he was able to walk round the whole island without stopping, resting or sleeping, and while Oroi was doing this she ran off with Te Ira-ka-tea. That

led to war between the tribes of Oroi and Hotamatua and as
the former was the more powerful there was nothing else for it
but for Hotumatua and his people to escape and seek a new
country if they wished to live.

At this time Hau-maka, who had tattooed Hotumatua, had
a dream in which his spirit travelled the sea and came to an
island where there were craters and a splendid coast on which
he saw six people landing at the same time. Hau-maka told his
dream to Hotumatua who realized that this was a prophetic
promise, so he selected six of his people, gave them a boat and
told them to keep going until they reached the land Hau-
maka's soul had seen. As they put out, Hotumatua called to
them: "Go and seek a strand worthy of receiving your king."

The six had a swift and easy voyage. It was to Te-pito-te-
henua they came and when they saw Rano Raraku, the
volcano, they cried: "There is Hau-maka's crater." And that
became the volcano's original name. Next they began sailing
round the island in search of the beach of which the king had
spoken. However, the beaches they saw were narrow and
studded with rocks and each time the leader of the six decided
that this one was still not worthy of the king.

Eventually they reached the place where today the village of
Anakena lies and when they saw the ribband of glorious sand
washed by calm green water, they all rose to their feet and
cried: "This is the beach of which Hau-maka dreamed. Here
our king shall dwell."

So they turned the bows of their craft towards the shore and
landed.

On the beach was a large turtle, asleep. They tried to turn it
over onto its back and in the tussle the turtle seriously
wounded one of them. The others picked the wounded man up
and carried him to the cave known as Ihu-arero. There they
remained for three days, tending the wounded man; then,
remembering the orders of Hotumatua they decided they
must make their way to the western coast and there await
their king. They did not, however, know what to do with the
wounded man, being ashamed to leave him to his fate. So, at
the entrance to the cave they built five tall mounds of stones,
telling them to reply in their names if the wounded man
should call them. They then went away.

They had scarcely got to Mataveri when they saw a large
boat approaching, which was in fact Hotumatua's two boats
lashed together. The king called to them from the boat asking
them what sort of land it was and they replied that it was not a

good land, for the fields were full of weeds and what weeds you pulled up grew again like lightning. Then the king uttered a spell; "Bad land, you shall be good during the ebb and the flood shall destroy you."

None who heard this understood its meaning. Some thought the curse applied to Maraerengo, which the sea was to swallow up; but one and all were afraid and they asked him why he had said that and whether he was not afraid his words would invite misfortune.

Then Hotumatua cut the ropes with which the two boats were lashed together and told Tau-ko-ihu to take one southwards along the coast, while he went north. The two boats reached Anakena at the same time; then seeing that the other boat was outdistancing him, Hotumatua from the bows of his boat shouted: "Oars don't pull!" And so great was his authority that Tau-ko-ihu's boat stopped dead and so Hotumatua was the first to step onto the sands of Anakena. Then he heard moaning: it was his wife in the pangs of labour. At once he summoned Tua-ko-ihu who saw to the delivery of the infant, reciting the spells that would bring it success and the grace of the gods. At that same time, as Tau-ko-ihu delivered the heir to the throne, his own wife brought a daughter into the world, the princess Avareipua.

That day all who had come with the king landed, bringing ashore the plants and animals they had brought with them. They came with *taros*, sweet potatoes, sugar-cane, *ti* and various trees, such as hibiscus and *toro-miro*, which later died. Of the animals only the rats and hens managed to survive. Hotumatua had set out with various other species, but they did not survive the voyage and some only reached the island when brought by the white men.

Oroi, to escape whom Hotumatua had left his homeland, had secretly sailed with him, bent on revenge, and he too came ashore under cover of night. For a long time Oroi roamed the length and breadth of the island, then one day he saw Hotumatua's sons lying face down resting in the sun after swimming. Tired, they fell asleep and then Oroi crept up on them and killed them.

That evening, Hotumatua, grown anxious by his sons' failure to return, set out in search of them. When he found their bodies on the beach, he looked all round carefully and, weeping bitterly, said:

"Oroi, you have crossed the sea to continue your war, for I see your hand in this."

A year passed during which Hotumatua travelled the
island, visiting the villages that were being built and taking
part in ceremonies, teaching his subjects the sacred songs of
their ancestors. Meanwhile Oroi followed hard on his heels,
waiting for an opportunity to kill the king. One day he
stretched a cord across the path of the king, but Hotumatua
saw it and trod it down. Oroi gave it a tug, but he failed to trip
the king and Hotumatua called to him: "Oroi, the day is
coming when you will die by my hand."

One day as Hotumatua was walking through Hanga-te-
tenga, Oroi again stretched a line across his path. The king
saw it on this occasion too, but he pretended to have tripped
and fell in the grass. When Oroi leaped forward to kill him,
the king jumped to his feet and smashed Oroi's head with his
club. That was how Oroi, king of Maraerenga, died. His body
was placed in an oven, but being a ruler his flesh could not be
eaten, so they carried his body to one of the *ahu* which still
bears his name.

When Hotumatua grew old, he divided the island among
his children, each of whom became the ancestor of the tribes
that were there when the white men came. Having made this
arrangement, Hotumatua went to the top of the volcano,
Rano Kao and sat down by the edge of the crater. For a long
time he gazed out to the west where lay the land of
Maraerenga he had left. He summoned the four gods that
inhabited the land of his fathers: Kuihi, Kuacha, Tongau and
Opapaku, and when they had come, he said to them: "The
time has come for the cock to crow."

Then the cock in Maraerenga crowed and its crow was
heard across the sea marking the hour of Hotumatua's death.
Then he turned to his sons: "Carry me hence," he said. And
they carried him to his hut and there he died. After his death,
his body was laid in the *ahu* near Akahanga.

Many years passed. The island then was ruled by a people
with long, pendant ears. It was these clever people who set up
all the *ahu* along the coast, the heavy labour being performed
by their slaves, a people with short ears.

One day the long-eared ones said to the short-eared: "Take
all the stones that stick out of the ground and throw them into
the sea." The short-eared replied: "We can never do that, for
we need the stones for cooking our potatoes, sugar-cane and
taros." The long-eared ones were furious over this
insubordination and decided to destroy the short-eared.

Not far from the promontory called Poiku, they dug a huge

trench that ran from the northern to the southern shore of the island. Then they filled it with dry branches intending to roast the short-eared ones. However, it so happened that a short-eared girl from Potu-te-rangi, called Moko-Pingei, had married a long-eared husband. None of the short-eared ones knew why this great trench had been dug and were even more surprised when it was filled with branches and dry grass. The short-eared girl pestered her husband with questions until he told her the purpose of the trench. That same evening the girl told this to her relations. It was decided that they should keep an eye on her house and she would signal to them when the long-eared ones started lighting the fire and then the short-eared could come up on them from behind and push them into the flames. It would then be the short-eared who would feast on the long-eared and not the other way round.

The girl returned home. When the time came, she went out in front of her house and waved a basket she held in her hand, this being the agreed signal. The short-eared ones then crept up on the long-eared ones as they were setting fire to the leaves and branches in the trench. Disconcerted by the suddenness of the attack, they did not even try to defend themselves, but fled. But where could they flee? They all fell into the flames — men, women and children — except for three of the warriors who escaped over the piles of bodies and ran off in the direction of Anakena where they took refuge in the cave called Ana-vai. The short-eared ones pursued them and used long poles to try and force them out of the cave. As they prodded, the three leaped from side to side uttering weird cries that made the short-eared roar with laughter. In the end, two of the three were killed. Then one of the *matato* went up to the men with the poles and told them to spare the survivor, there being no reason to kill him. After this the short-eared went back to the great trench where the bodies of the long-eared were still burning and filled it in with earth. They then went home and ever since they have been the sole masters of the island. When the surviving long-eared warrior was dragged from the cave, he cried out in terror: "*Orro, orro orro!*" using a language the short-eared did not understand; so they called him Ororoina and a man called Pipi Horeko took charge of him. Eventually, he took a short-eared woman of the Haoa family as his wife and they founded the family of that name, which has provided the present headman of the island.

Unfortunately that was not the end of the island's troubles. There was a great war, but whether that was shortly after the death of Hotumatua or before the appearance of the white man no one knows. However, in it many were killed and even today if you walk about the island you will come across their bones among the stones and rocks.

King Maurata did not live to take part in the return to Easter Island. He died on Chincha in 1864. Some years later, however, a handful of the survivors among whom were members of the royal family, did return to Easter Island and there their descendents still live, proud of their ancestry and ready to boast of it to visiting scientists. That, however, is all they have, for the royal family never recovered its authority and the rule of the descendents of Hotumatua ended more than a hundred years ago, and with it that chapter of the island's tragic history.

X

ENTER BROTHER EYRAUD

At the beginning of May 1863 Father Pacôme Olivier, Provincial of the Congregation of the Sacred Heart in the Chilean port of Valparaiso, heard a knock on the door of his cell just as he had finished his daily breviary. The door opened and in the doorway, lit by the rays of the setting sun that were making their way through a narrow gothic window, was the stocky figure of a monk of about forty. His name was Brother Eyraud and he had come because he had heard that it was Father Olivier's intention to found a new mission on Easter Island and he asked if he might be allowed to join the mission and accompany Father Albert to the island. He sounded full of enthusiasm and eagerness, both qualities that appealed to the Provincial, who asked Eyraud to tell him about himself.

He was told that Eugene Eyraud was born on 5th February 1820 in the French Alps, the son of a poor farmer who had difficulty in feeding his family of eight sons. Shortly afterwards two of the eight died and Eugene himself, then scarcely two, was seriously ill, but recovered. Then, when he was nine, his mother died. Ever since he could remember, he had dreamed of being able to study, but the family's resources would not allow for more than one to be educated and the eldest was given the chance. Then, however, Eugene received a letter from his godfather, who was a locksmith, suggesting that he go to Blois and learn his trade. Bundling up his few belongings and with 100 francs from his father in his pocket, Eugene set out on foot from his native village of Champsaur, down the Drac valley heading for Grenoble and Lyon.

For the next couple of years he learned to be a locksmith. The a prosperous emigrant offered to put him in charge of a locksmith's business he had started in distant Argentine, but before Eyraud got there, the business was destroyed by enemy action. Having no means and no job, he took work in a hotel. After four months of this, he set off through the Cordilleras and Andes, a hard and dangerous journey, hoping to reach the Pacific. That was how he came to Chile. He started locksmith's businesses in Santiago, Valparaiso and Copiapo. When, in 1847, his older brother Jean wrote to him that he was becoming a priest, Eugene was able to send him 600 francs. Two years later, he got a further letter from his brother, then one from China where he had gone as a missionary.

After this his own aim in life was to become a missionary himself. One day, while working in his workshop in Copiapo, through the window he saw two priests of obvious French appearance standing in the street. It turned out that they were members of the Congregation of the Sacred Heart and it was on their initiative that in 1856 he began his novitiate, which he interrupted after ten months to make a short visit to France to see his family. He then returned, finished his novitiate and here he now was asking the Provincial to allow him to fulfil his ambition.

Only a few days after this conversation Eugene Eyraud went with Father Albert Montinon and Father Clair aboard the schooner, *Favorite*, which then set sail for Tahiti, arriving on 11th May 1863. Tahiti was a French colony. In Papeete, the capital, the Vice-Provincial of the Congregation, Father Fougue, told him that in the town were four men, a woman and a child from Easter Island. When the Peruvian slavers had extended their activities to Tahitian waters, the French governor had gone into action, capturing several of them. He also let the inhabitants of the Marquesas and Tuamoto know about them, so that, when the slavers came there, the brave inhabitants let themselves be enticed aboard and disarmed the crew. Then they sailed the ship to Tahiti and handed the slavers over to the French authorities. The six Easter Islanders had been in the ship in question.

At about this time, on the initiative of the Bishop of Oceania, Jaussen, the French chargé d'affaires in Lima entered an energetic diplomatic protest about the activities of Peruvian pirates, demanding the repatriation of Polynesians from the guano islands. Of these only about a hundred still survived, disease, hunger and the ghastly working conditions having killed off the rest.

On the voyage it was discovered that one of those being repatriated had smallpox. The resulting epidemic killed seventy-five with the result that only fifteen returned to Easter Island after their two years of bondage. Their return proved fatal to the other Easter Islanders, for they brought smallpox with them and the islanders died like flies. Starving dogs dragged the bodies of the unburied dead away, further spreading the disease.

This tragic news reached Papeete while the three missionaries were there, serving as yet another incentive. Yet, as it transpired, neither Father Albert nor Father Clair were able to go and the task of organizing the mission was entrusted to Eugene Eyraud, who set about the preparations with great energy. He managed to get together several pieces of percale, carpenters' tools, four corner-posts and planks with which to build a house on that timberless island, a barrel of flour, three catechisms in Tahitian and a small bell with which to summon a congregation. All this was loaded into the schooner *Suerte* and on 9th December, 1863 Brother Eyraud left Papeete for Easter Island taking with him the six who had been rescued from the Peruvian slavers and who, he hoped, could help by interpreting. With him, too, he had a young Christian from Mangareva, called Daniel, who was his assistant.

Suerte touched at the Gambier archipelago, where they took aboard five sheep and slips of trees they hoped could be acclimatized and grown on Easter Island.

After a voyage of twenty-four days, they made landfall on 2nd January, 1864. There were really only three places where they and their goods could be landed: Anakena bay in the north, Hanga Roa in the south-west and Vaihu in the south. Brother Eyraud was eager to land at Anakena, as that was where, less than a century before, the Spaniards had performed their ceremony of taking possession of the island. After a brief consultation with the captain, the six islanders were asked to come on deck and questioned as to the best way. After slight hesitation, due to the distance at which the island still lay, they all said: Anakena and pointed towards it.

In case the people on the island should be taking them for pirates, the captain did not go close in, but put the islanders into the ship's boat and told them to row ashore and tell their friends there of the white man's friendly intentions.

Since early that morning Brother Eyraud had had a severe headache, so as soon as the ship's boat had departed, he went below to his cabin and lay down. He was woken from his sleep by the thump of bare feet overhead and the sound of voices all over the ship. He hurried on deck thinking something had happened and that the islanders had returned unexpectedly. It turned out, however, that while he slept the captain, considering Anakena too shallow for landing, had on his own initiative altered the plan and set sail for Hanga Roa. He assured Eyraud that for four pieces of percale the islanders would be more than happy to carry all his things across the island to Anakena.

Brother Eyraud accepted the position, having no choice, and towards evening the schooner reached Hanga Roa. As darkness was falling and sounding becoming difficult, it was decided to postpone landing until the following morning.

The next day was a Sunday. Daniel was sent ashore to reconnoitre. Daniel, of course, was their linguist. He knew several Polynesian dialects, quite good French, and English. Although he did not know the language of the Easter Islanders, it was sufficiently close to the Polynesian for him to be able to make himself understood. It was not long before Daniel was back on board and highly indignant. Apparently he considered the Easter Islanders dreadful people and would not go back on shore for a thousand piastres. The islanders had been armed with spears with which they had threatened him. Many of them had been completely naked. Their feather ornaments, tattooing and savage cries had frightened him.

After some discussion it was decided to land Brother Eyraud and one of the islanders called Pana at Hanga Roa and that they would go overland to Anakena. Meanwhile the ship would sail back to Anakena and wait for them there to unload their baggage.

When Brother Eyraud found himself ashore, he at once understood Daniel's fright and realized that he had been too ready to accuse him of cowardice. On the shore was a dense throng of men, women and children numbering, he estimated, some 1200. The men held primitive spears consisting of a straight stick with a head made of a pointed piece of stone. He could not help being surprised by the fact that unlike the other Polynesians many of the Easter Islanders had European features and light, almost white skins. Daniel had said that the crowd had been all men and Eyraud found it easy to see how he had made the mistake, for both sexes wore similar tapas wound round their bodies and you had to look a second time to distinguish which were the women, mostly by the way they did their hair and by their head ornaments.

Although in a hurry to be gone, Eyraud scrutinized the throng searching for the islanders whom they had landed at Anakena the previous day. In the end, he did see them, but was disconcerted to find that they behaved as if he was a perfect stranger and paid not the least attention to what he said. Another thing that surprised him was that the other islanders seemed not at all interested in the sudden reappearance of those the French had rescued, let alone delighted to see them back. The only thing in which they showed any interest was the few possessions of the rescued men; then the crowd turned its attention to the belongings of Eyraud and Pana who had great difficulty in preventing them being taken.

Feeling that he was not going to be able to force his way through the throng, Eyraud wondered whether he had not better go back to the ship and sail in her to Anakena, so rather desperately he began signalling to the captain, waving his hat and scarf. His signals were not understood and the schooner drew away quickly, becoming smaller and smaller and finally going down below the horizon. Eyraud was now quite at the mercy of the islanders and ahead of him lay some four miles of hills before he could reach Pana's native village, where he could hope for hospitality from the latter's family. Meanwhile, he was being troubled by hunger and evening was at hand. Fortunately Pana was able to enlist the help of some men in the midst of whom they were able to make their way through the throng and then as darkness fell, set out for the village. The going was rough and difficult. The men kept urging Eyraud to greater speed. By about eleven o'clock he was at the end of his strength and the men agreed to shelter in a small cave to which two local women brought a few roast potatoes.

The next morning they set out again and reached Anakena about noon. As they came to the bay, they saw the ship coming sailing in. Eyraud waved to the captain to bring his ship in, yet he did not seem to understand. Eyraud ran along the shore, followed by a crowd of islanders and the ship. When he turned back, so did the ship. In the end, unable to communicate with the missionary ashore, the captain headed out to sea again and the ship disappeared. Eyraud was overcome with despair. There he was on the island alone without food or the most elementary necessities. His only comfort, which was not a great one, was the discovery of Pana's hut and family, from whom Eyraud eventually learned that the captain had sailed back to Cook's Bay and there unloaded all the missionary's effects. This news was both comforting and disturbing, for the excessive interest the islanders had taken in his few possessions was still too fresh in Eyraud's memory for him not to fear what might happen to all the things the ship had landed. Having been on the go more or less the whole of the night, he was not fit to set out again, especially as his feet were blistered. As Pana's family had invited him to spend the night in their hut, he decided to accept.

Some roast potatoes made him feel more himself and he again took an interest in his surroundings. This visit to an islander's home made such a deep impression on him that he devoted part of the report he sent to the Bishop of Tahiti to it:

> This was the first visit I had ever paid to a kanak's hut. I wish you to see it with me and my description shall not be too long. First the furnishing: unusually simple and modest, comprising a gourd acting as a water-carrier, a small bag of plaited straw for carrying potatoes. You will be better able to understand the appearance of the bed and furniture, if I first describe the interior of the hut itself. Imagine a crustacean half-open and balanced on the two halves of its shell and you have a picture of the hut's shape. Its roof consists of a few sticks covered with straw. A tiny opening like a stovepipe allows people to crawl inside, not on hands and knees, but on their bellies. This 'door' is in the middle of the building and admits enough light for people to be able to recognize each other after they have been inside a short while. It is difficult to imagine the numbers that can find shelter beneath one such thatch.
>
> It is very hot inside the hut. Even that would be perfectly tolerable were it not for the squabbling resulting from the inhabitants' lack of ideas of hygiene and their communal ownership of most goods. None of the many inhabitants of the hut will leave it without taking with him all his clothes and possessions, if any. At night, however, there being no other shelter, they all act alike. They take their place on the floor in such position as conditions allow. The door in the middle of the hut provides an axis dividing it in half. Along this axis and on either side of it, everyone lies down head to head with just sufficient space between them for anyone coming in or going out to pass along. Thus people lie athwart the hut making themselves as comfortable for the night as they can.
>
> Tired though I was, there was too much to keep me from sleeping and thus I was able to listen to the songs and the sobs which, as I was told are the kanakas' expressions of enchantment.
>
> With the dawn the first object that I made out in the hut was the little domestic idol,[1] to which, as I observed, no one paid much attention.[2]

---

[1] Later visitors maintain that Eyraud is wrong. Statuettes in these huts are not idols nor do they have any religious character.
[2] Eugene Eyraud: *Rapport sur l'Ile de Pacques*. Annales de la Propagation de la Foi, Lyon 1860-1867. Vols. 38 and 39.

Early the next morning Brother Eyraud set out to go back to Hanga Roa hoping to recover his things that had been unloaded there. When he reached the shore, he found a crowd of islanders already there, tightly thronging round the heap of his goods and chattels. Some men armed with spears were guarding his chests and heavier goods and his building materials, but his loose possessions and personal belongings, not in padlocked containers, were already in the hands of the islanders, who made no attempt to disguise the fact of having taken them. One, indeed, was going about wearing his hat on his head, while another had put on his coat. Nonetheless Brother Eyraud was so delighted to see that his equipment had been landed at last that he made no attempt to recover these trifles but confined his efforts to his heavy luggage.

What had caused the biggest sensation and was giving rise to considerable discussion was the four posts intended to support the roof of his house. Some of the islanders said that these were boats and other guesses were made. Eyraud turned their interest to good account and employed a slight subterfuge to recover his possessions. He gave the crowd to understand that if they would given him access to his things, he would show them the use of the mysterious posts. This was agreed and he was let through. Eyraud then took up hammer and nails and set to work. Only then did the islanders realize that the timber was intended for a house.

Brother Eyraud was not altogether pleased by the choice or rather the lack of choice of a site for his mission building; but once it was finished it was a great relief to have all his belongings under lock and key and he looked forward to sleeping under his own roof. Scarcely had he stretched out on his bed, clutching the keys in his hand, when he suddenly saw a huge figure standing in the doorway. This was Temanu who had brought him three chickens. This was Eyraud's first real friendly contact with the islanders. Almost immediately afterwards another islander appeared, Torometi, dark-skinned, influential, and the future protector of the mission. He walked straight in and, holding out his hands, demanded that he be given the chickens "to relieve you of bother and to cook them." The demand was made in a tone that made refusal impossible and the missionary did as he was told, thereby finding a protector and a master, for Torometi was to care for and exercise authority over the missionary for all the nine months and nine days that he spent on the island. Torometi more or less fed him and seems to have regarded him as his property in much the same way as the Roman patricians did their educated Greek slaves.

Living next door to the missionary, he was a constant visitor, if that word can be used of an association so unceremonious. He would walk in at any hour of the day or night, lie down, move things about, generally behaving as if he was at home there.

Torometi was about thirty, tall and strong for an islander; he looked distrustful and suspicious and his reputation was not of the best. The others, in fact, shunned him, proclaiming him to have come from some other island. Yet nonetheless he had made himself a de facto leader of the Easter islanders. One morning he appeared in the missionary's cabin and made him open all his boxes and cases one by one. He rummaged through them all and finally seemed to have set his heart on a small metal hatchet and this, without asking, he just stuck in his belt. When the missionary ventured to make a mild protest, he was told: "If you need it, I'll lend it to you."

Torometi never parted with the hatchet and other objects in the missionary's possession soon went the same way. Torometi's real desire was to possess the big bell with which three times a day the missionary summoned the islanders to prayer and to be taught the catechism. Brother Eyraud was able to save his bell, but only by parting with a small service bell, the sound of which thereafter could be heard in all the various parts of the island to which Torometi went.

Not having to worry about his domestic economy, Brother Eyraud was able to devote himself to his missionary work, mainly religious instruction. In spare moments he tried to discover how the islanders lived and what their social problems were. As he reported to his superiors, the islanders had no real work to do at all. One day's exertion assured them of a year's supply of potatoes. The other 364 days of the year they spent walking about, sleeping and visiting. There were continual gatherings and holidays. When one finished at one end of the island, another began at the other end, only the nature of the festival changing with the time of year. In the spring were two months of Mataveri celebrations, which included races and competitions. Often their celebrations were so prolonged that they merged with the following celebration of Paina.

Paina was the great summer festival, during which banquets were held. Autumn and winter are the rainy seasons on Easter Island and the time when the festival of *Areauti* is

Rock drawings and bas relief of *tangata-manu* from the rocky slopes of the village of Orongo and the offshore islands. Each was made after the discovery of the first *manu-tara* egg of the year

Various drawings of the man-bird, *tangata-manu*

held. Most competitions and races are held during Areauti:
there are singing and poetry contests etc. During one of these,
some islanders took five lambs belonging to Brother Eyraud
and roasted them. The delicious meat was long celebrated in
song.

One day Eyraud, tired of Torometi's continual thefts,
decided to frighten him — with the prospect of hell. First,
however, he had to explain that there was a life after death.
Scarcely, however, had he pronounced the words *E pohe oe*
(you will have to die) than Torometi went green in the face
and began to shake like a leaf. Then, recovering somewhat, he
ran from the cabin in panic. Within a short time the whole
village knew that Papa had pronounced *E pohe oe* over
Torometi, and everyone drew away from the poor missionary
as if he had done something improper, though he was never to
discover what, or why the words *E pohe oe* had had such an
effect.

On another occasion while he was giving a catechism
lesson, a ship was observed on the horizon, a rare sight in that
out of the way part of the world. Brother Eyraud interrupted
the lesson and went to his cabin to make preparations in case
the ship came to the island. When he emerged from his cabin,
the islanders asked him if he had been talking with the ship
and what it had told him.

As he roamed the island visiting the islanders in their huts,
Brother Eyraud made an interesting discovery: in every hut
there was a wooden tablet or stick covered with hieroglyphs in
the shape of animals not then present on the island. These
hieroglyphs were carved with sharpened stones. Each figure
had its own name, but as the tablets were seldom used,
Eyraud felt that though the tablets may have been of primitive
texts, the present islanders made so little use of them, that
they no longer knew what the hieroglyphs meant.

In the days of Brother Eyraud, the islanders could grow
their crops almost without effort. Though stony, the soil was
sufficiently fertile not to require manuring and the regularity
of the rains made irrigation unnecessary. Potatoes being the
only crop the islanders grew, their work was considerably
simplified. All they did was to make a hole in the soil with a
stick and into it drop a seed potato. The only other labour was
the harvesting of the crop. Potatoes were really the only item
in the diet of the Easter Islanders. Roasted in the Polynesian
manner in holes in the ground filled with heated stones, these
potatoes were delicious, but eaten exclusively day after day

even they were apt to pall. The only other item of the Easter Islanders' diet was chicken, reserved for special occasions. Surprisingly enough, fish was scarcely ever eaten or caught. Another curious observation Brother Eyraud made was the revulsion felt by the sight of blood. Once when he cut the head off a chicken he was intending to cook, one of the women who happened to see the trickle of blood, fled in panic. When the islanders killed an animal, they strangled it. They used their hands to deal with a chicken, but when wanting to kill a dog or a goat, they dug a hole into which they thrust the animal's head, then covered it with earth and waited for it to suffocate. They then burned off the hair and cooked the meat with the potatoes.

Brother Eyraud had various squabbles with the otherwise peaceable, good-natured islanders, some of which were quite serious. The main cause seems to have been Torometi, whose appetite was whetted by each successive object he got the missionary to part with. If the missionary withdrew into his cabin, Torometi would gather together all the people of the village and they would sit down round the cabin at a distance of some fifty paces. If Eyraud did not react to this, they would begin throwing stones at the cabin, at first just a few small stones, but ending by pelting it with quite big stones. Usually after such a demonstration, Eyraud gave way and let Torometi have what he wanted, because he expected that otherwise the outcome might be very unpleasant. It was not that his life was in any real danger, but he knew that such a bombardment was usually the introduction to setting fire to the hut being pelted, as he had seen the islanders do when quarrelling among themselves. Otherwise they never struck or killed each other.

One of Brother Eyraud's dreams was that he should build a little chapel in which he could give religious instruction during the rainy season. In fine weather he always taught the catechism in the open. This dream was not an easy thing to bring about for in that part of the island the only building material was clay, but Brother Eyraud set about making bricks by mixing clay and straw and drying them in the sun. It was hard work and a task in which he received no help, for Torometi had refused to lend a hand and the others seemed to have no interest in building at all.

After making a quantity of bricks, Eyraud marked out a rectangle 8 metres by 4 metres. He dug a rough foundation and began the walls. When those had risen to a height of 1.30

from whom you've been brought back. You'll soon find out about that, however, for it's all over between us. You may take your things and go back to those people, who won't give you even one potato to eat."

Torometi's attitude was a great surprise to Brother Eyraud, but it left him with no alternative but to take his things and move to Hango Piko.

Torometi's prophecy proved correct, for within a week Eyraud had had every one of his things stolen. That, however, was only the first of the misfortunes that now assailed the poor missionary. Plundered of practically everything he possessed, he returned to the mission cabin at Hanga Roa. It was now September and the time for Mataveri was approaching. This festival began with a great meeting of the inhabitants held at a place over a mile from the missionary's cabin and which Eyraud jokingly called to himself the Champ de Mars. Torometi watched the preparations for the meeting with evident disquiet. His main opponent, Tamateka, explained to Eyraud that practically everyone hated Torometi and they would express their hatred at the meeting.

A few days later, Eyraud was able to watch from the window how Tamateka at the head of a crowd of his people surrounded Torometi's hut, tore off its thatch and set fire to it. In a moment the whole hut was ablaze and Eyraud darted outside, afraid of the danger to his own cabin which was quite near Torometi's hut, from which a gusty wind was sending smoke and sparks swirling straight at the mission. However, he found that men with spears were on guard to keep the flames from spreading.

Meanwhile Torometi was standing there watching with stoic resignation. Then one of his few friends drew him aside. Shortly afterwards the crowd became aware of the boat that Torometi's people had salvaged, and leaving the burning hut to look after itself, ran to it. Torometi took advantage of the confusion to start edging out of things. So far, Eyraud had been a passive observer, but he now decided that the moment had come for him to declare himself for one side or the other. In view of the disastrous effects of his leaving Torometi, he decided now to join him. In a moment the two were the centre of a billowing throng. Then Eyraud felt someone snatch his hat from his head, then his coat was stripped off him, his waistcoat, his boots, etc. until he was standing there so incompletely clad that there was little difference in dress between him and the islanders. Looking round, he saw his various garments and other pieces of his breviary being sported by various islanders. Unable to get out of the crowd, he was carried along with it until, thanks to Torometi's physical strength, he was enabled to escape and got back to the cabin, from which he wished to rescue a few things before leaving the village. Having lost the key with his clothes, they had to get inside through the chimney. This time, the missionary let Torometi have whatever he wanted. So, taking what they could, the two men set off for Hanga Piko, where Torometi's brother lived. There they spent the night and continued the next day to Vaihu, Torometi being afraid of pursuit. As it turned out, his fears were fully justified, for when they got to Hanga Piko they learned that Torometi's brother's hut had also been burned.

The people of Vaihu were more hospitable and friendly and Eyraud continued his work there. After a week, his new pupils brought the exciting news that there was a ship on the horizon. This proved to be a large sailing-ship, but as she was heading south, Eyraud presumed that like the four or five other ships sighted while he had been on the island, she would sail past without calling and, disappointed he returned to the daily round. The next day, however, at about eight o'clock a boy came running to the missionary with the news that the ship was anchored in Hanga Roa and that Torometi, who had already gone back to his village, requested him to come there as quickly as possible.

The village was in a state of great excitement. The islanders were afraid the ship might be in the hands of pirates or slavers, but Eyraud seeing that she carried the French flag, reassured them and himself went aboard the *Teresa Ramos* to be met by Captain P. Barnabe. On 30th October 1864, he reached the coast of Chile after spending more than nine months on Easter Island.

At a rough wooden table in a dimly-lit hut sat a figure in a soutane writing a letter, apparently oblivious to the thuds of objects striking the iron roof. The door and shutters were tightly shut and bolted. The only light came from a small oil lamp. The letter the man was writing was addressed to Father Pacôme Oliviera, Provincial of the Congregation of the Sacred Heart, Valparaiso, Chile. The writer was Father Hippolite Roussel, born in La Ferté-Macé in France, who had gone as a missionary to Oceania in 1854 and who was to die on the island of Gambier in 1897, after spending some time on Easter Island. In his letter he wrote:

There is no question of our closing an eye whether by day or
night. These grown-up children surround our hut singing,
shouting, banging on the tin roof and pelting it now and then
with stones. Everything has to be securely shut. For the last two
months we have been forced to light our lamp at midday if we are
to say our breviary. If I do have to go outside, I am surrounded by
a throng, whose intentions are all too obvious and just awaiting a
good moment to rob me. I come back to find the lock filled with
gravel, so that I cannot insert my key.

It was on 25th March 1866 that Captain Gambier in *Notre
Dame de Paix* had put in to Hanga Roa. Though several weeks
had now passed since the inhabitants of the cabin on Easter
Island had landed, their situation had not improved. Three
days after its arrival, the ship sailed again leaving on the shore
Father Hippolite Roussel, Brother Eugene Eyraud and three
baptized islanders from Mangareva.

The moment that Brother Eyraud had heard that Father
Roussel was intending to found a permanent Catholic Mission
on Easter Island, he had volunteered for work there. He had
longed to go back almost since the moment he had left it,
despite his experiences there. Then, nearly two years later, the
opportunity had come.

Remembering how he had lived in constant fear lest the
islanders set fire to his cabin, Eyraud this time took with him
several sheets of corrugated iron for the roof of the mission
house. The precaution was fully justified: from the moment
the missionaries landed the islanders exhibited the most
obvious desire to strip them of their possessions. A crowd of
them surrounded the cabin the missionaries had built for
themselves day and night, denying anyone access to it, and
this continued for almost six months. Finally the missionaries
realized that being confined idle in a tin fortress got them
nowhere and that they must do something. They then began
going outside and talking to the islanders through the three
interpreters from Mangareva they had brought with them and
whose language the Easter Islanders understood. After some
time, the islanders had become so accustomed to the presence
of the missionaries that the latter were able to start building a
proper mission house and begin actual missionary work.

Brother Eyraud was the builder. With the three from
Mangareva to help him he built three adjoining houses round
the three sides of a largish rectangle, the fourth side of which,
facing the sea, was closed with a palisade. In this they sowed
various seeds and planted the bushes and shrubs they had

104   *Island of Secrets*

brought with them. One of these buildings served as a chapel, the others as dwelling quarters for the missionaries and the islanders. (The chapel stands to this very day some 500 metres from the shore).

The missionaries tried to win over the Easter Islanders, but the latter, remembering the wrongs and misfortunes the white men had caused them in the past, were suspicious and sometimes even hostile. Eyraud had no advantage from being on good terms with Torometi, who had now lost all authority with the islanders and was quite without influence; while the attitude of his previous competitor, Roma, who had replaced him, was decidedly hostile.

Father Roussel found other ways of winning the confidence of the islanders and introducing Christianity among them. Fate had destroyed the island's hereditary monarchy, yet the islanders still had a sentimental attachment to the all but extinct royal family which was now quite without authority. Discovering that there was an orphaned son of the last king who was both unusually quick and intelligent, the missionaries concentrated all their energies on this fourteen-year old boy, Kerekorio. They took him to live at the mission, taught him the catechism and finally baptized him, hoping that the solemn ceremony would have the effect on the islanders that they wanted. However, to the great disappointment of the missionaries, Kerekorio died in 1867, ruining all their plans.

During his first stay on the island, Eyraud had vainly tried to fathom the system under which the island was governed. He had watched and even played an involuntary part in the conflict between Torometi and Roma, but he had never known what decided who was leader and he was not to discover this until his second visit.

Early in the spring, usually in September, the contestants for power went to the interior of the island, where they spent six or even eight weeks searching — for the nests of a rare bird. The one who first found one of these nests would be chosen leader. This sounds a relatively easy task, but in fact during his more than nine month's stay in the island, Eyraud only once saw one of these rare birds. This selection process was said to have been in use since time immemorial.*

*This is really the same procedure as that described in Chapter 8 concerning the sacred bird, the differences in detail being due either to inaccuracies in the missionaries' account or perhaps that the procedure was re-introduced by the islanders after their return from exile.

On 6th November 1866 *Tampico* arrived at Easter Island bringing two more missionaries from Valparaiso, Gaspard Zumbohm and Theodale Escolan. These two brought with them a cow and a horse, two animals that had never before been seen on the island. The mission expanded and put up more buildings.

On 14th February, 1868 the first mass baptism of 380 islanders took place. However, neither baptism nor religious teaching were of benefit to the islanders whose standard of living remained as low as ever. There is no doubt, however, that the missionaries' activities caused irreplaceable loss to learning, for they fanatically destroyed all the wooden tablets, called *rongo-rongo*, with their mysterious hieroglyphs, burning them en masse.

On 19th August, 1868 Eyraud died and was buried on the island. The others continued his apostolic work though not always using his methods.

As always in the history of colonization, after the missionaries come the traders and exploiters, and so it was in the case of Easter Island. The captain of *Tampico*, Dutroux-Bornier, settled in the island and 'bought' from the naive islanders a considerable area of land for which he paid a few pieces of cloth. When the islanders, quite ignorant of what the transaction involved, wished to return to their fields, Bornier denied them access and threatened to use arms. After a time he went to Tahiti, whence the local entrepreneur, an Englishman called Brander, suggested that they joined forces to exploit the possibilities of Easter Island and Bornier returned to the island as representative of the new company.

On his return he found the population in the ferment of the struggle for leadership. The protagonists were Torometi, trying to recover his old position, and the villagers of Hanga Roa. On 15th April, 1870, there was a decisive struggle between the two forces. On that day the sound of cannon fire was heard on the island for the first time in living memory. It was fired by Bornier who had decided that the internecine strife was a threat to his business and so he fired a shot from the cannon he had brought back with him into the midst of the fighting throng. The islanders were outraged and turned against the white man in their midst, destroying his houses and boat. Fratricidal fighting continued all June and July. In it Torometi killed his own brothers: Teoni, Daniel and Mihi. On 7th July the islanders smashed Brother Eyraud's tomb. To the missionaries' disgust, Bornier took an active part in the slaughter, firing indiscriminately at the islanders. On his orders the village of Hanga Roa was burned on 10th July and on 22nd July he is recorded as having fired at Father Roussel. The protests and pleas of the missionaries and of Bishop Jaussen proved of no avail. The slaughter continued until the end of February 1871. At the end of April of that year, realizing that Bornier was deaf to all their arguments, the Bishop ordered the closing of the mission and the transfer of the missionaries to Gambier Island. With the missionaries went the last brake on his conduct and Bornier loaded 300 of the islanders into a ship and sent them to his partner, Brander, in Tahiti, for forced labour on his plantations there. When the missionaries left the island, many of the islanders, realizing what fate awaited them, tried to go with them, but only a few were able to do so. Bornier was able to compel 175 to leave the ship and go and work for him.

Of the 300 Easter Islanders sent to the plantations of Haapape on Tahiti, 250 died within a short time. Of those left in the island itself, only 111 were still alive six years later. The population of Easter Island was thus close to extinction.

Meanwhile, however, the island's executioner, Bornier, himself died. The cause of death was never properly established, but there is little doubt that he died a violent death. Some say he was kicked to death by the horse, others that this victims skewered him on his own bayonet. He left a widow, an island woman called Koreto, and two girls of five and six. After her husband's death, Koreto began to act as if she were queen and her daughters heir to the throne.

Later, Brander's new partner and agent, a man called Salmon, arrived on Easter Island. He moved into the missionaries' former house and used the church as a warehouse. Salmon expanded the farming that Bornier had begun and within a short time he had built up the herd to 600 and had a flock of 1800 sheep.

By 1936, Williamson and Balfour, the firm which had taken over from Brander, were running 40,000 sheep on the island and these produced sixty to seventy tons of wool a year.

Violence and lawlessness were more or less inevitable because the island was ownerless, no state or other government claiming it. The colonial powers were then busy squabbling over the division of Africa and had no interest in so small an area lost in such a vast expanse of ocean. The French missionaries made several vain attempts to get their government and the governor of Tahiti to take an interest in

Easter Island, even suggesting that France should annex it.

In the end it was Chile that took an interest in this masterless island, to which it was, of course, the nearest country and on 9th September, 1888 Chile formerly took possession of Easter Island. For a long time, however, this was no more than a paper formality, which is not so surprising when it is remembered that the island lies nearly two and a half thousand miles from its metropolis.

Though the island was now theoretically ruled by Chile, in 1897 a new exploiter appeared on the horizon. This was a Chilean entrepreneur from Valparaiso, called Merlet, and it was not long before he had all but 1391 hectares of the island's land under his control. The protests and arguments of the islanders, who said that they were threatened with extermination, received the stereotyped answer of the bureaucracy, that the whole island had been bought from the government and that if the islanders wanted land to cultivate they could sow their crops round their houses. Elsewhere on the island there was no land available for them. Not only that, but the agent of the new company told the islanders that he would pursue and imprison anyone who took water from Tahai (the nearest source of water fit for drinking) as its water was reserved for the company's animals.

The only way for the islanders not to starve to death was to buy food from the Company, which sold sheep for 10 pesos each and cattle for 100 pesos. The only way in which the islander could get the cash to pay these prices was, of course, to work for the Company. Doing this, they could earn 20 centavos a day, that is: they had to do 50 days work for a sheep and 500 days for a bullock.

The naive islanders were easy victims for the wiles of the white man, not for the first time. At the funeral feast for an eminent islander they ate two bullocks and ten sheep (altogether 1500 days work). On another occasion they ate 30 sheep (1500 days work) and innumerable head of poultry, thus more or less selling themselves into slavery.

Thus the bugbear of the nineteenth and twentieth centuries came to Easter Island at the same time as scholars began taking an increased interest in its vanishing culture.

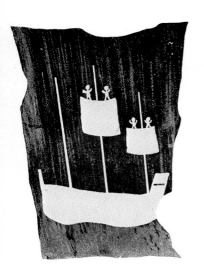

(*above*) Drawings on the inner walls of the stone dwellings of Orongo representing European sailing ships and discovered by Geiseler's expedition; (*below*) Entrance to the stone dwellings of Orongo

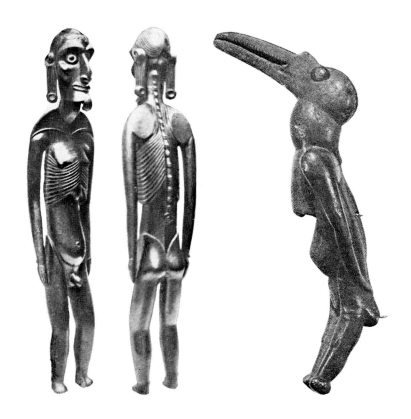

(*above*) Small wooden and stone carvings made by Easter Island artists; (*below*) One of the mysterious carved hands brought from Easter Island

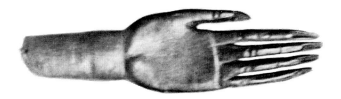

that the learned call *bustrefedon*.¹ Then he had another surprise.
When the youth had stopped singing, the Bishop pointed to
one of the hieroglyphs and asked him how to pronounce it and
what it meant. Yet to the Bishop's astonishment Metoro, who
had just been able to sing the entire text, was quite unable to
interpret individual hieroglyphs. Scrutinizing the tablet,
Jaussen saw that on every other line the hieroglyphs were
reversed, standing head to head, and at these places the
motive of the song was repeated. Further investigation showed
that the hieroglyphs were really ideographs, more exactly,
curiologics, that is to say that each individual sign stands for
an object. This left the question: if this really was writing on
the tablet, how did the individual signs combine to make a
logical whole expressing thought or thoughts?

The further he delved, the more the Bishop became inclined
to suspect that the signs were not writing, but fragments of a
form of writing whose origins and meaning were lost in the
mists of time. All the tablets sent by Roussel were of relatively
recent manufacture while the island's culture was obviously in
a state of utmost decline, and the Bishop found it difficult to
forgive the missionaries for burning so many of the tablets in
the mission stove, suspecting that which had been destroyed
might have held the clue to the hieroglyphs' meaning. This
suspicion was further confirmed by the fact, as Metoro told
him, that the *Kahau rongo-rongo* were used when they had
gathered in a circle to sing their songs. It was not that they
knew the meaning of the individual signs; but they knew the
songs by heart, these being handed down from one generation
to another, but they served to remind them of the verses and
thus each tablet was a sort of prompter.

Metoro could not explain the meaning of the individual
hieroglyphs, though he could recite the entire text of the song;
thus the hieroglyphs must have had some meaning to him,
though not enough to call it reading. What connection was
there between hieroglyph and meaning? It was this that
Jaussen now tried to discover. First, he sent to Roussel asking
him to see if there was anyone among his Easter Islanders who
could still recite or sing the texts of the wooden tablets and if
so, to try and write these down. It proved, however, that none
of the survivors could do this. Not one of the younger
generation, who were the only survivors, any longer knew the

¹ From two Greek words *bous*, ox, and *strephein* — to turn, meaning like a ploughing
ox. The oldest Greek and Italian writing was in this zigzag pattern: one line from left
to right, the next from right to left, and so on.

old songs that hitherto had been passed down from generation
to generation.

The Bishop realized that his four tablets were a real
treasure and an academic puzzle and this latter he determined
to try and solve. Once more he and Metoro got down to work.
Metoro recited the text of each tablet over and over again
while the Bishop noted it down word by word and in this way
eventually achieved a phonetic rendering of the text of each
tablet. Not knowing the Easter Island language he had to ask
Roussel for the dictionary he had compiled during his short
stay on the island. The Bishop and Metoro then began the
task of attaching a phonetically written word to the correct
sign, separating words and signs that were repeated and
placing them in groups. This was a laborious task and, as
Jaussen admits, did not guarantee that the results were
accurate.

The final result was a thirty page booklet which the Bishop
later published and which is a sort of general vocabulary of the
hieroglyphs of Easter Island. Jaussen still regarded the signs
as bustrefedon and curiologic. The hieroglyphs are divided
into fourteen basic groups and meanings are given for some
500 of them. The wooden tablet in his possession he named
thus:

La Rame (the oar)   90 centimetres x 10 centimetres with
                                 8 lines on each side and a total of
                                 1547 signs

Le Bois Enchancre
(the curved wood)   40 centimetres x 15 centimetres with
                                 10 lines on one side and 12 on the
                                 other, totalling 1135 signs.

Vermoulue (the rotten)   9 lines on one side, eight on the
                                 other, with a total of 822 signs.

Le Miro   29 centimetres x 20 centimetres
                                 having 14 lines on either side and a
                                 total of 806 signs.

Thus Jaussen had a total of 4310 signs to examine. The
notes of his sessions with Metoro occupy over 200 pages
which, perhaps, gives a better idea of the labour involved in
producing the 30-page booklet, which he sent to centres of
study of oriental languages in Manila, Borneo, Batavia and
Nossy-Bé. This resulted in a flood of requests for further

information and material, as well as material sent to him for comparison, especially samples of other bustrefedon curiologics. Of these the one with the most similarity to the Easter Island hieroglyphs was the signs carved in stone by the inhabitants of the Celebes. Out of these Jaussen developed a theory of the origins of the Easter Islanders, namely that they had come there some thousand years ago from the Malayan archipelago.

No one has yet completed the Bishop's work and the mystery of the Easter Island hieroglyphs remains.

XII

THE VISIT OF *THE HYENA*

A few weeks before *Hyena* was due to sail for Samoa, the western part of which was to become a German colony in 1899, the Admiralty in Berlin received a request from the head of the Ethnographic Department of the Imperial Museum that on her way from Valparaiso the gunboat should call at Easter Island to make certain scientific studies and collect specimens for German museums. The request was granted and in June 1882 *Hyena's* commander, Captain Geiseler, received orders to put in at Easter Island and there make various studies as instructed by Professor Bastian, head of the Ethnographic Department.

Captain Geiseler was not an academic nor did he have any scientists among his crew, but *Befehl ist Befehl* and the Admiralty's order had to be carried out. With few to choose from Captain Geiseler detailed an aspirant called Weisser for the duty and handed him the Professor's written instructions. That done, he heaved a sigh of relief and told himself that he had fulfilled the first part of his orders.

Weisser set about his task with enthusiasm and real German thoroughness. Knowing nothing of the subject, the moment the gunboat reached Valparaiso Weisser set out in search of literature and information about Easter Island. Unfortunately there was little that he could obtain, but he did read the papers in which Professor Philippi, Director of the Chilean Museum in Santiago, recorded the results of his examination of the writing on the *rongo-rongo* tablets that he had brought back from Easter Island in 1870. He also read some works on the mysterious stone columns and it was with this slight equipment that he set about completing the task entrusted to him.

Just before *Hyena* set sail, the German consul in Chile arrived and presented Captain Geiseler with a copy of the English map of the island of 1870 on which were recorded the latest information and the measurements of the coastline made by the Chilean ship *O'Higgins*. So, on 19th September, the German gunboat reached Easter Island and that same evening anchored off the village of Vaihu.

The following morning Geiseler and Weisser were put ashore, landing at a spot where they had observed a fire burning the previous evening. There they encountered a group of men on horses, one of these being a European. On introducing themselves, it proved that the man they had taken to be European, was in fact a halfblood Tahitian called Salmon who had charge of the island's economy after the violent death of Dutroux-Bornier in 1876. He gave the Germans a most hospitable welcome and offered them all assistance, an offer which they soon discovered to be more than a polite formula, for during the several days the Germans spent on the island, he supplied them with provisions, water, labour and personally acted as their guide.

Salmon was then almost the uncrowned king of Easter Island. He was related to the former royal family of Tahiti and revered accordingly by the Easter Islanders, whose mainstay and support he was. Although he exploited them almost as badly as his predecessor had done, the islanders were grateful to him just for not being Dutroux-Bornier. He was a partner in the firm of Brander and quickly increased the livestock on Easter Island to 12,000 sheep, 700 cattle and 70 horses. He sent to Tahiti some 20 tons of wool a year. Having a complete monopoly of trade on the island, he had introduced a new system of paying the islanders for their work in cash, while they had to buy all their tobacco, tools and other luxuries and necessities from him at his own very high prices.

The Germans sailed round the island and made further landings at Hanga Piko and elsewhere. Weisser and his companions made their way through the interior to Mataveri and made various other excursions, among them ascents of the extinct volcanoes Rano Kao and Rano Rarku. As instructed, the Germans tried to collect as many exhibits as they could for their museums at home. This was not easy, as it was impossible to transport the best exhibits which were the enormous stone statues.

At the foot of Mount Topaze the Germans discovered an intriguing stone bust that appeared to be part of some pagan idol. As this was small, at any rate by comparison, they bought it off the islanders for the low price of 30 dollars. Twelve men dug it out and they got ropes and levers to try and transfer it to the ship. However, they had not moved it more

than a few yards before they realized that the task was beyond
the strength of the crew and to their great regret they had to
give up the idea and leave it on the island. The deal was called
off and the islanders asked to return the purchase price.

The Germans could not understand how the primitive
islanders, who had neither machinery nor the most
elementary tools, had been able to carve and then transport
and erect statues weighing many tons. Unable to take them
away, Weisser set about sketching them and other carvings he
found, making full use of his time on the island. Not only that,
but he walked every road and track on the island, climbed the
extinct volcanoes, went down into their craters and many of
the subterranean caverns; he visited villages, talked with the
islanders, listened to the tales Salmon had to tell about the
habits and customs of the islanders, making hurried notes of it
all. All this was included in Captain Geiseler's report to the
Admiralty and later published with maps and drawings.
Weisser had been scrupulously attentive to his instructions
and had not only described, but measured the height and
girth of the statues and even of their individual parts: nose,
ears, etc. The biggest he measured was 23 metres high: its
head measured 11 metres, the nose 3.80 metres, while the face
was 3.40 metres across and the chest 3 metres.

For a few dollars Weisser bought the islanders' agreement
to his excavating a few old graves and removing the skulls and
bones for anthropological study at home.

On his way about the island Weisser came across several
groups of stone foundations of ruined houses. One and all
were in the shape of a long boat pointed at either end. These
were probably the remains of the former villages of Hanga
Roa, Hotu Iti and Terano, mentioned in the reports of earlier
expeditions and which presumably had been destroyed during
the time of civil strife and raiding by slavers. Near these
villages he found numerous graves, some of them quite
imposing and piled with stones. As all the districts that
Weisser visited were owned by someone and the owners were
never slow to make requests for a fee by signs, the Germans
were continually having to put their hands in their pockets
and buy permission to examine and take away exhibits.

There was one of the islanders who claimed to own an
imposing grave and required considerable persuasion to open
it for them. The interior looked like the last resting place of a
chief, but it contained only a human skull and a few bones,
plus a lot of skeletons of birds. When these latter were pointed

out to him, the islander began uttering owl-like cries and, gesturing, gave them to understand that the birds had come in by mistake through two openings in the wall and, being unable to find a way out, had perished.

When asked the significance of these openings in the wall the islander had explained that they were to enable the spirit of the dead person to get out. When asked why there were two openings, he explained that one was a reserve exit in case the god Make-Make should try to persecute or kill the spirit. From this grave Weisser took a sample of dressed stone from the quarry in the crater of Rano Raraku.

Possibly the most interesting and original discovery made by the Germans was that of the old stone huts on the slopes of Rano Raraku, where Weisser found a number of unusually interesting stone bas-reliefs of which he made accurate drawings.

On 21st September *Hyena* moved to the bay of Hanga Piko. After a brief stay in the village of Mataveri, the Germans continued on towards Rano Kao, taking the northern side, as the southern falls steeply into the sea and forms one of the three sharp promontories of this triangular island, which is so similar in shape to Sicily that some people have called it "the

Stone tomb at the foot of Rano Raraku, as drawn by Weisser

Sicily of the Pacific". The crater of the extinct volcano, Rano
Kao, is some 250 metres deep and is almost completely round
with a circumference of three and a half kilometres. The base
is covered with water, forming a small lake to which several
trodden paths lead from the rim, these having been made by
cattle going to drink. Finding nothing noteworthy inside the
crater, Weisser and his group climbed out and followed a
narrow path along the rim on the western slope of the volcano,
where, according to Salmon and the islanders, they would find
the ruins of old houses. And, indeed, they soon came across a
pile of stones that at first sight seemed to have been piled up
higgledy-piggledy, but on closer inspection they distinguished
the ruins of individual stone huts, each of which looked like a
mound of large stones. They made their way inside one of
these through a narrow opening some six feet long measuring
20 inches by 24 inches. Having crawled in with some
difficulty, they found themselves in almost complete darkness.
The stone roof was so low that they could only crouch as they
examined the interior by the faint light of matches. On the
side opposite the entrance were some stone tablets covered
with drawings executed in red, white and black. These were so
interesting that they decided to try and get inside the other
huts perched in a semicircle on the narrow shelf of rock on the
volcano's side that fell steeply to the sea. Here and there in the
jumble of stones they could see figures and bas-reliefs that
seemed to be idols.

It was already late in the day and there was not sufficient
time to sketch the carvings and drawings, nor light enough
inside, so they decided to return to Mataveri and come back
the following day. On the way back they came across yet
another stone hut that they had not examined. The stone slab
that served as its roof being split they were able to get inside
comparatively easily and there on the wall they found a
relatively well-preserved carving of the head of some weird
idol. Being unable to take it with them, Weisser sketched it by
the light falling in through the roof.

That same evening, after they had returned on board, the
gunboat sailed to nearby Vaihu where, at Salmon's request,
the villagers organized dances and sang the old songs for the
visitors. Early the next morning, the Germans went ashore at
Vaihu and began the ascent of Rano Kao only this time up the
path across Orito. As they were passing through the old,
abandoned settlement of Vinapu they came across a jumble of
volcanic tufa that apparently had once been stone statues,

Bas relief of a deity discovered by Geiseler on the inner wall of one of the stone dwellings of Orongo

only now so weathered and damaged that it was scarcely possible to guess their original shapes or features.

Having reached the huts where they had been the previous day, they set about measuring them. The first was 9.60 metres long and 1.45 metres high. The entrance corridor measured 2.45 metres long by 0.55 high and 0.50 wide. The interior was 7.10 metres by 2.50 metres and 1.60 metres high in the centre and 1.30 metres at the sides. On the wall opposite the entrance were two stone bas-reliefs measuring 94 by 34 by 25 centimetres, covered with figures. It was so damp inside that the colours were quite soft and could easily be smudged with the fingers. The same painted reliefs were found in the other huts they investigated. The figures represented not only idols, but people, boats and even an old European sailing-ship. Many of them repeated an identical motif of a bird, which they knew as the object of a special island cult. In another of the huts they found a strange drawing which the islanders said was of a god called Oreo-Oreo. Both the carvings and the drawings were so fragile and friable due to long action of damp that there was no question of taking any with them, so

Weisser made a whole series of sketches and also a map showing their exact position. He also tried to discover what purpose these abandoned huts had served and was told that they were shelters used by egg-collectors during a few weeks of the year.

As well as a god of fertility the islanders since time immemorial had venerated Make-Make, a sort of supreme deity. His symbol was the egg of the sea-bird that nested on Motu Nui, a tiny island a few hundred yards only to the west of Rano Kao. The eggs of this bird were strictly tabu except during July, August and September when you were allowed to gather them. Before the introduction by the Europeans of poultry, the eggs of sea-birds had constituted an important item in the Easter Islanders' diet and also a luxury. It was thus no wonder that the most daring and agile swam across to Motu Nui, Motu Iti and Motu Kao, where most of the nests were. The searchers set out from the exposed rim of the extinct crater and so the islanders had built there a row of stone huts to provide the swimmers with shelter. This place was named Orongo. The lowness of the entrances was explained as a measure of defence.

The collection of the eggs called for no little exertion, daring and agility, for the collectors not only had to swim across several hundred yards of turbulent eddying water but then climb the side of the volcano which was 1000-1200 feet high and almost sheer. Again it was not surprising that jealous searchers sometimes came to blows over their collections. This explained in part the discovery of long clubs shaped like eels and ending in a curved head with open jaws that were used to repel an attacker trying to enter a hut.

The huts were used mainly at night but also at times of great heat. The Germans came to the conclusion that the drawings and carvings on the huts were more or less contemporary with the giant statues scattered all over the island.

On their return to Mataveri the Germans hired horses to transport their specimens to Hanga Roa and the next day bought further objects from the islanders in Vaihu. Thus, for all the shortness of their stay, the Germans returned to Europe with a rich store. Captain Geiseler's report has attached to it a list of 87 different objects obtained for museums. They included a number of wooden and stone carved idols, king's sceptres, primitive tools such as stone hammers for carving, woven materials, nets, weapons, ornaments, clothing and a

whole case of skulls and human bones. What they discovered
threw considerably more light on the legendary celebrations of
the Sacred Bird.

XIII

AN AMERICAN EXPEDITION

Early on 18th December 1886, a Saturday, the American ship *Mohican* dropped anchor in Cook Bay. She had to sail again for Valparaiso on the last day of the year, so all those who had come to do scientific research were in a hurry to get ashore and start work. Scarcely had the anchor dropped than Salmon and Brander, who happened to be in the island, came aboard to offer their help and services while practically all the rest of the island's population lined the shore of the bay, first the men, then at a safer distance the women and children.

A crowd followed Brander and the Americans after they had come ashore and were walking the mile to Brander's house where the Americans deposited their baggage, tools and instruments. That afternoon they made a first reconnaissance of the crater of Rano Kao and visited the old stone huts in nearby Orongo. Then, they mounted Salmon's light carriage and were taken to his residence at Vaihu, where a great surprise awaited them.

It transpired that not only was Salmon a valuable source of information about the island, almost a walking encyclopaedia, but also a knowledgeable collector of its antiquities. During the many years he had spent on the island he had been able to make a valuable collection of things that had belonged to the former inhabitants. The Americans spent most of their first night on the island cataloguing the items and trying to persuade the owner to sell certain of them, both duplicates and quite a number of originals. The finest of these latter was undoubtedly the original 'talking wood' tablets, the famous *Kohau rongo-rongo*, with their mysterious hieroglyphs.

Early the next day, the Americans set out for the island's central plateau that is surrounded by the mountainous Teraai, Punapau and Tuatapu, this being where the quarries are from which came the red tufa with which the head-coverings of the huge stone statues were made. Then they climbed Rano Kao, taking the south-west path, and, following the rim of the crater above the waters of the lake at the bottom, they soon arrived at the village of stone huts, Orongo. These straggled along the outer rim of the crater. Their shape and situation being dictated by the space available on the narrow shelf of rock running round the crater and below which the side drops more or less sheer to the sea.

No sooner had they reached the village, than they set to work examining the insides of the huts. They sketched and copied the stone ornaments and decorations until faced with the question of whether to return to Vaihu for the night or spend it up there in the stone huts. Although the latter procedure would have enabled them to make an earlier start, the insides of the huts were so damp and musty due to the lack of ventilation that the Americans preferred to make the laborious climb to the village again the following morning rather than spend the night at Orongo. The evening was well spent even so, writing down the texts of local legends and stories in Salmon's translation.

At first light on Monday, 20th December, the group set out a second time for Orongo, on this occasion taking eight sailors from the ship to help in unblocking the entrances to some of the huts, moving stones and digging. One of the greatest difficulties was crawling down the narrow corridors into the huts and more than one person underestimated his girth, got stuck and had to be pulled free by his feet.

With proper tools and light they were able to work well and quickly, the only unpleasant factors being the damp, the mustiness and the stench from the soft damp earthen floor.

They counted 49 huts of varying shapes and dimensions. The largest measured some 13 metres long, three were 10 metres long and eight about 6.5 metres. Most were single rooms, but there were some with two, even three rooms.

Roughly in the middle of this huddle of huts was a sort of open space onto which faced the openings of eight hut entrances. On investigation they discovered that these eight huts were all connected with the others by long passages. Another, somewhat smaller space similarly surrounded by intercommunicating huts was discovered at the end of the line of huts. In front of the entrance to each hut, about three metres out, was a small hollow in the ground about a foot square in which were traces of the fires at which the inhabitants presumably had cooked their food. The islanders' method of preparing food had always been very primitive, that of lighting a fire in a hollow filled with stones and then, when

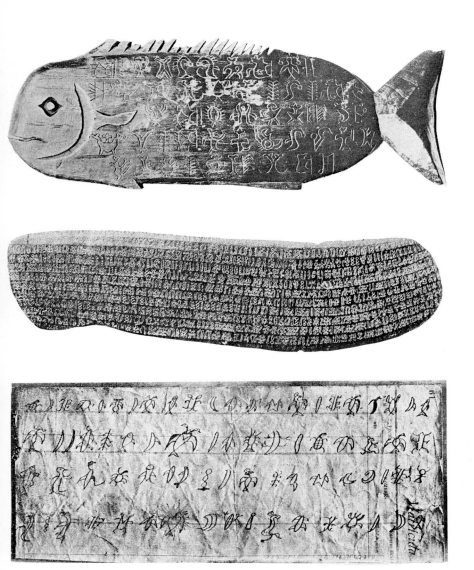

(*top*) Two examples of *kohau rongo-rongo*, the wooden tablets of various shapes covered with hieroglyphs; (*bottom*) Fragment of Tomeniki's book

(*above*) The W. Mulloy expedition reconstructing the Akiwi *ahu* using the islanders' traditional method; (*left*) Raising statues using modern means

depressions in the hard volcanic base of the shore. These were eliptical, almost round and undoubtedly the work of human hands. They were about one metre in diameter and more than 50 centimetres deep. Most lay above the high-water mark, but others almost exactly on it, so that they were filled at high tide. The only explanation of them that the Americans could think of was that these had been made as storage tanks for live fish.

A little further on they came across a stone tower, some four metres in diameter and nearly seven metres high. According to the islanders this had been built as an observation post for their turtle hunting. At the foot of the tower, as near every older building on the island, the Americans found quantities of human remains buried at various times and in various stages of decomposition. Some of the older skeletons crumbled to powder on encountering the air when they were brought to the surface. It seemed that the whole island was one great cemetery. Wherever you dug, there was a grave. The most frequent site for burying the dead seemed to be in the vicinity of those stone platforms and also the natural caves in the rocks, of which there were many all over the island.

The Americans devoted special attention and time to investigating the stone platforms in many of which they found catacombs and tombs containing quantities of very old skeletons. Many of the bases of the old statues were still in position on the platforms. Most of these bases were irregular in shape, though some were quadrilateral and one octagonal.

At one beach, just by the sea, between two of these platforms they found a carefully laid stone floor sloping gently down to the sea which at this point bristled with protruding and submerged rocks. However, straight out from this laid floor was a narrow channel leading safely through the rocks to the open sea. It appeared to be a port and an ideal landing place for boats. Some of the Americans advanced the suggestion that the stone colossi could have been brought by sea and landed there. This idea was soon dismissed, however, as so far there had been no evidence of the islanders ever being capable of building boats or rafts of the requisite size. And of what could they have built them, when there were no trees on the island?

When they got to Cape Ahuakapu the Americans found a capacious and interesting grotto in which were the remains of numbers of people and animals, especially marine animals. The walls of the grotto were covered with simple drawings of

boats, fish and people in various attitudes. Not far away was
another stone platform and another observation tower
somewhat shorter than the one near Anakoirangaroa.

Above Camp Mohican, on the slopes of Kotatake, they
found the ruins of an old settlement. This extended for close
on two kilometres and was undoubtedly the oldest settlement
on the island. All that remained was the foundations of its oval
houses. It was so old that the islanders really knew nothing
about it, not even its name. Neither Salmon nor Brander had
ever been in that half-desert part of the island and so they, too,
had no information to give about it.

Investigation did not reveal much about the past of the
settlement either, for time had played havoc with it all. The
foundations were of unknown stone and in the back wall of
each was a curved niche built of lava. These were undoubtedly
domestic altars like those found at Orongo, differing only in
that their construction was very much more primitive.

After two days' hard work the Americans returned to the
shore. A bathe in the sea at dawn and a hearty breakfast of
lamb that had been cooking all night on hot stones, local
fashion, put the Americans on their feet again and it was
decided to continue their march round the island.

On 23rd December the Americans began exploring the
southern coast of the island, starting at Anakena (La
Perouse). They soon discovered that the whole of that part of
the coast and its immediate hinterland was peppered with
stone platforms, old tombs, ruins of stone huts dating to
different periods in the island's history and in varying stages
of dilapidation. Many of the platforms were partially
dismantled, as later generations of islanders had taken stone
from them to build their homes. In some of the islanders'
homes the Americans saw stone bas-reliefs in the walls that
could only have come from those old monuments.

The greater number of ruins and their concentration there
showed that previously and for many centuries the bay must
have been the main cultural centre of the island and perhaps
also its capital. Legend had it that this was where the first
chief of Easter Island, Hotumatua, and his adherents had
landed. What puzzled the Americans, however, was where the
inhabitants of this undoubtedly once populous settlement had
obtained their drinking water, for this part of the island was so
arid as to be almost a desert.

Close to the village of Anakena they discovered a large stone
statue in an excellent state of preservation. They were told
that this was a female figure and the last work of a generation

pieces of sculpture scattered about the outside of the crater.

Still more difficult was the erection of a statue on a platform, *ahu*. These platforms had their base specially lowered at the back to facilitate erection of the statue. An inclined plane of earth was first built and up this the statue was rolled and then erected on the stone plinth with the aid of ropes. When all its statues had been rolled up and onto the platform, the earth ramp was removed. The whole process called for enormous labour, and was only possible because of the numbers engaged and their skill.[1]

On 27th December the Americans went to a second and larger mason's workshop on the west face of the crater. Here they counted 155 statues in various stages of work. It was here they found the giant, still unfinished statue already mentioned that measured more than 20 metres. As they examined the various statues the Americans noticed that one of these had a strange indentation round its neck and what seemed to be the marks of an attempt to cut off its head. The islanders confirmed that this was what had happened, explaining that according to the legend this statue had belonged to the clan that lost the war. In order to bring their defeat home to the losers, their victorious opponents had tried to cut the head off their statue. It is difficult to know what truth there is in this, but it sounds probable. The islanders called this statue Hia-ra (meaning: How many there?) The Americans discovered that each platform and each statue on it had a name and the islanders were perfectly familiar with them all.

Whereas the stone platforms had obviously served as tombs and catacomb, the Americans found nothing of interest under the single statues.

On 28th December the Americans started excavating the foundations of the masons' dwellings in the two quarries, which they had discovered, close to the mason's yards-cum-quarries inside the crater. There were the ruins of several stone huts like those we have already described. The Americans thought it possible that the Easter Islanders might have been accustomed to bury their valuables below the threshold of their houses, like the Red Indians did; however they found nothing except one rectangular flat stone with a carved outline of Make-Make, the favourite motif of the rock-carvings at Orongo. This one stone was found at a depth of one metre at the entrance to the largest of the houses; in front

---

[1] Later expeditions have put forward other suggestions for the technique used in erecting these statues.

of which was an extensive stone terrace.

During the excavations in the crater one of the islanders produced from some hiding place three human skulls and brought them to Thomson. Once he had been paid lavishly for them, he told them they had come from the platform called the King's Platform, where legend had it, used to be the tomb of the island's kings. The Americans were amazed to see that on the front of each skill had been carved a miniature Make-Make.

A further small mason's yard, previously overlooked, was found on the outside face of Rano Raraku. This contained some fifteen relatively small statues.

The whole stretch of the volcano's side down to the village of Vaihu was peppered with tumbled statues lying face down. At first the Americans supposed that the statues were being transported when something suddenly interrupted the work, but if that was the case, why were they transporting the statues face down?

In one group of three statues was one that was obviously that of a woman. Her face and breasts were overgrown with moss with the result that from a distance they appeared to have been coloured green.

The Americans made further excavations on the slopes of Rano Raraku from their base at Vaihu. They visited Orito where the islanders obtained obsidian for spear-heads and carving instruments and where they dug the clay they mixed with juice from the sugar cane to make a red paint.

The enormous amount of carving that must have been done is demonstrated by the fact that the Americans counted 555 large statues, the largest over 20 metres tall and the smallest 90 centimetres. These were all made of grey trachyte which is porous and relatively easy to work with the stone tools the Easter Islanders had. Being as soft as sandstone, it is also not very enduring and easily affected by the atmosphere.

The islanders not only had names for each statue, but attributed supernatural attributes to them. They were supposed to move about during the hours of darkness discreetly rendering aid to their clan by casting spells, laying curses etc. One story is that the creator of the first statue was Tuii-ko-iho, a son of the sixteenth king, Mahuta Ariiki,[1] who died before his father. There is no way of establishing when this was, as the journals of the early visitors to the island do

[1] King Mahuta is not mentioned by either Tepano Jaussen, Father Roussel nor yet by Lappelin.

not mention it. It is probable that at the time of Cook's visit to Easter Island, the quarries and masons were still active, only, unfortunately, none of the members of that expedition got to Rano Raraku.

Dimensions apart, whether one metre high or twenty-five, the statues are all almost identical in design. The head of each is immensely elongated, the eyes are set close together and deep in their sockets with beetling brows; the nose is big, but flat and the nostrils are flared; the upper lip is short, the lower protruding. The angle of vision is slightly upwards, the expression of the face grave, as though deep in thought. The Americans made no mention of the eye-sockets of the statues ever being filled with artificial eyes of bone or obsidian as was the case with the islanders' wooden statues.[1]

The top of each statue's head was made flat as if to provide a surface on which to put a stone hat of red volcanic tufa. The statues round the crater which the Americans examined were much flatter-bodied than those on the platforms by the shore. They almost looked as if they had been mass-produced. There were outline-figures of humans from the waist up and cut straight at the waist to provide a solid base on which it could stand. The face was the only feature properly carved, while the hands were merely indicated in relief on the torso. Every statue had elongated ears that proved characteristic and as later, more careful examination was to prove, the older the statue, the larger its ears.

As far as they could make out from the islanders, these statues were monuments to eminent members of the island society and their purpose was to immortalize their memory. They had never been regarded as idols nor formed part of a religious cult. For religious purposes the islanders' had their guardian spirits, gods and goddesses, represented in tiny wooden or stone carvings that had no connection at all with the huge statues on stone platforms.

The sculptors of the huge statues had formed a privileged class. Their craft was hereditary in the male line and to be a member of a sculptor's family was as much a matter of pride as the possession of royal blood. One of the Americans' guides was one of the former and never lost an opportunity of emphasizing that one of his ancestors was Knu-rau-ta-hui, a famous sculptor.

What must have been a matter of particular difficulty was

---

[1] Some scholars maintain that in ancient times these statues had beautifully-made artificial eyes with irises of mother-of-pearl and pupils of black obsidian.

the placing of the red tufa hat on the head of the statue after it had been erected. These hats came from the mountain Teraai, where lots had been found in various stages of manufacture. Being cylindrical, they were relatively easy to transport, indeed they could just be rolled to their destination. This tufa is relatively soft and light and easy to work. The specific gravity of volcanic tufa is 1.4, while that of the stone used to make the actual statues is about 2.1. The largest hat found was 3.81 metres in diameter. Their average weight was about 3 tons, which is much less than that of the statues. One must remember, however, that this not inconsiderable weight had to be hoisted to no mean height to get it into place. To accomplish this another inclined plane of earth and stone was built leading to the top of the statue and up this the cylinder was rolled. Once it was in place on the statue's head, the incline was dismantled, the earth being used for gardens and the stones to strengthen the foundations.

The dimensions of the platforms varied considerably, but they all had common features and an identical purpose. Many were in an excellent state, even though all the statues had been toppled off them. Others again, presented a picture of complete destruction. Most of the platforms were sited along the shore close to the sea.

The structure of the platforms was relatively simple, though requiring lots of labour. The outer walls were built of rectangular, carefully-dressed stones that fitted exactly and were joined without the use of cement or clay. The inner walls were built parallel to the outer walls but of unhewn stone, the space between the two walls serving as a tomb. The rear wall was considerably lower than the front, falling gently towards the ballast; some were finished off with a few stone steps.

The Americans came to the conclusion that the destruction of the platforms when the statues had been toppled higgledy-piggedly was the work of nature: an earthquake or volcanic eruption. This supposition appeared to be borne out by the disorderly scattering of statues at the quarries and dispersal of tools looking at though they had been flung down in sudden panic and not as a result of being gradually abandoned. Against this theory, however, is the fact that there is no mention in island tradition of any volcanic activity or earthquakes. When the Americans tried to question the islanders, explaining that a volcano is a mountain with a crater in which is smoke and fire, the disbelieving islanders shook their heads asking how there could be fire in a crater, which is a place where there is water.

As they went about the island the Americans catalogued a total of 113 stone platforms, obtained names for each and where possible recorded its history and gave its measurements. Here are some entries from Thomson's catalogue:

Platform No. 1. — native name *Hanga Roa*. Only the bare remains: 18 m. long, 2 m. wide. The surface stone was taken by the missionaries to build their mission.

Platform No. 2. — *Ana Koiroraroa*, 30 m. long, 3.81 m. wide, 3 m. high. The outside stones untouched, the inner scattered in disorder relatively recently, probably by islanders putting the bodies of their dead inside. Judging by the position of the statues toppled from the platform, these had stood facing inland with their backs to the sea. All the statues were in a very bad state, one completely destroyed, another had been broken by falling, a third had lost its head, on its neck were obvious traces of a saw. As it transpired, some years before a French warship visiting the island had removed the head.

Platform No. 6. — *Anotai*, 36.5 m. long, 5.35 m. wide, 2-3 m. high, in a very bad state. One of the toppled statues had in its back a deep hollow the purpose and origins of which have not been discovered. Excavation revealed human remains and interesting objects.

Platform No. 9. — *Kitui Kihiraumea*, 56.7 m. long, 2.7 m. wide, 2.75 m. high. The central part made of splendidly hewn, polished stones. Four toppled statues in a good state. Skulls, spearheads and stone tools obtained from the ruins.

Platform No. 11. — *Hananakoa*, length 75 m., width 3.65 m. and height 2.75 m. Well preserved, built of very large stones. Traces of carving difficult to decipher on the front. Inside are well-built catacombs and tombs containing remains so old they crumbled on contact with the air. Removal of one stone revealed a heap of human skulls, with unusually wide, powerful lower jaws. Most striking was the fact that there was no sign of other parts of the body. Judging by its dimensions and the solidity of its construction one could conclude that it was intended to carry one of the largest statues which was lying not far away.

Platform No. 15. — called *Hanga-ta-riri* (meaning 'hostile words'). Length 31.4 m., width 3.35 m., height 1.82 m. Very bad state, but some polished frontal stones are still in position. Four of the statues are lying face down, two others have fallen with their backs to the sea. At a distance of some metres was found a tomb measuring 15.25 m. by 1.83 m. built comparatively recently of hewn stone taken from the platform. One of these stones has some badly-worn hieroglyphs carved on it. Several hundred metres further away on some grass was a huge statue lying face down. Everything points to its having been destined for erection on this platform yet it seemed to have been suddenly abandoned while being transported there. Later generations have dug out under the statue turning the statue itself into the roof of an earth-like cave.

Platform No. 36. — called *Maru* (meaning 'peace'). Overall length 91.5 m. Central part 21.33 m. long, 2.13 m. wide and 2.43 m. high.

Platform No. 52. — called *Tongariki* (the north-west wind), the largest in the island. 164.5 m. long, 2.75 m. wide and 2.44 m. high. Graced with 15 giant statues all toppled inwards and then smashed on the stone base. Nearby lay the broken red cylinders that had been on the statues' heads. One of the central foundations of the platform had been built of red tufa carved into the shape of a human head.

The Americans spent two days on this platform, removing the frontal stones one by one in order to gain access to the graves and catacombs inside. Inside, in the centre, was a narrow corridor full of human remains. The oldest, main tomb had been walled up and had presumably been built before the platform was made.

The surviving stones showed that the statues had been sited symmetrically, equidistant one from the other. The entire plain behind Tongariki Bay was one huge cemetery in which were the graves of thousands of people. Although the islands were officially Christian they still preferred to bury their dead there, even at the time of the Americans' visit.

Platform No. 82. — *Motu-o-pope*. 114.3 m. long, 3 m. wide and 2.13 m. high. Important because the six statues that had stood there all had short ears, the only ones ever found that did so.

Platform No. 109 — *Takiri*. Only largish, but attracting attention by its unusual construction. The Easter Islanders neither knew about cement nor used clay to join stones together. The walls of these platforms were built of huge volcanic stones weighing up to 5 tons. These were carefully smoothed and any cavity filled with small stones with the result that each wall presented an almost smooth surface. It is even possible that originally any holes were filled with sand moistened with water.

The care given to the finish of this platform would seem to indicate that it had been of particular significance and it is not surprising that most time was devoted to investigating it. Inside, however, they found nothing worthy of notice, apart from the remains of people buried relatively recently.

According to the islanders, this platform was the last to have been built and it was intended for the huge 21.5 metre statue found still unfinished in the quarry at Rano Raraku. Legend had it that as the platform and statue were approaching completion, the powerful clan Vinapu held a great feast to celebrate the coming event. The wife of the chief of the Vinapu came from the Tongariki clan. It so happened that during the festivities, whether accidentally or on purpose is not known, she was killed and her flesh eaten at the feast. At these feasts certain parts were the privilege of the various digitaries and not to be given yours was an insult. Legend has it that such a misunderstanding was made in serving out the woman's body and one of those thus insulted appealed for help to her clan! Hearing what had happened, the members of the Tongariki moved as one man to avenge the honour of their clan. This, apparently, was what began the long and bloody war that led to the destruction of the statues and caused the death of most of the great sculptors and platform-builders who also became involved in the internecine strife.

Platform 110. — *Vinapu*. The same construction and dimensions as the preceding. Immediately behind it is a circular earthen rampart surrounding a flat area of about 68.5 metres. Apparently this used to be an arena and a place for the great occasions. Excavations both inside and outside the rampart produced nothing.

Platform 112. — *Ahurikiriki* is at the south-west fringe of the island, sited on a protruding shelf of rock half way down a sheer drop of 300 metres to the sea. Here lie 16 statues in an excellent state of preservation. Though relatively small, it is scarcely probably that they could have been lowered on ropes. At some time there must have been a land route to the shelf that has since been washed away.

Platform 113. — *Kaokaoe*. Must once have been of imposing dimensions, but it has been almost completely removed by an islander who took the stone to help build a wall round his property.

William Thomson and the others in the American expedition were equally interested in the Easter Island writing and the mysterious *kohau rongo-rongo* tablets which by then had become famous in academic circles. Many expeditions had mentioned them even before the missionaries had turned their attention to them. Some' had made attempts to purchase them, but the islanders had asked such inflated prices that no one had been able to afford to buy one. The 300 islanders Brander had taken to Tahiti had several with them and these they prized, but no one then had been interested or wanted to buy them.

In January 1870 a Chilean corvette, *O'Higgins*, had visited the island and her captain, Gana, had obtained three tablets, two of which he gave to the National Museum in Santiago. The third he had sent to France, but it never reached its destination and all trace of it has been lost. Copies of the hieroglyphs on the Chilean tablets were sent to a number of museums in Europe. They aroused considerable interest in the Royal Anthropological Institute while Berlin considered they must be blocks for printing patterns on the local cloth.

When *Mohican* dropped anchor at Tahiti, Bishop Jaussen had at least seven tablets in his possession and these he put at the Americans' disposal. They had come to the Bishop via the missionaries on Easter Island and were all in an excellent state of preservation, so that the Americans were able to take really clear photographs of them. Prints of these photographs they took with them to Easter Island. While on the island, they showed these photographs to the islanders who, one and all, refused to admit the possession of any such things. It transpired later that Salmon knew of the existence of two and after much bargaining the Americans were able to buy them off him at a very high price.

These two tablets were not in the best state of preservation. One had been made of driftwood and its strange shape showed that it had once been part of a ship's boat. How this had come about was that one of the islanders, seeing how the missionaries were wasting valuable wood burning it in their kitchen stoves, got the idea of making a boat out of the tablets. When the ties loosened and it fell to pieces, he hid the odd bits and it was not till some time later that this particular piece came into Salmon's hands. The other tablet was made of toromiro, a local kind of wood.

When questioned about what had happened to all the other tablets, the islanders explained that the missionaries had given categorical orders that they were all to be burned, evidently thinking this would help rid the islanders of their pagan beliefs and ties with their ancient traditions, which they supposed to be recorded on the tablets. It is impossible even to guess at the extent of the loss caused by such idiocy.

According to legend, Hotumatua had brought with him to the island sixty-seven tablets. He was the first king to know the art of reading and writing. These sixty-seven tablets contained the history, genealogy and proverbs of Maraerenga from which Hotumatua and his subjects came. Knowledge of reading and writing was restricted to the royal family and the chieftains of the six regions into which the king divided the island and their sons and to the elected priests and teachers. Once a year the entire population assembled at Anakena Bay to listen to the reading of the tablets. This festival was of such importance that even the war was interrupted for it.

The same events that led to the destruction of the statues and the abandonment of the art of carving probably put an end to the carving of hieroglyphs as well. This is rather borne out by the age of the surviving tablets which corresponds pretty well with that of the unfinished statues found in the quarries. Nonetheless people knew how to read them up to 1862 when Peruvian slavers carried off the population.

Later, when the survivors returned to Easter Island, an attempt was made to revive the old traditions linked with the tablets. This, however, was halted by the interference of the Catholic missionaries with the result that when the Americans were at work there most of the islanders were ignorant of the cult connected with the tablets.

Having bought the two tablets the Americans asked the islanders to read and translate them. One old man, Ure Vaciko, who claimed to have studied the hieroglyphs while in exile in Peru and still to understand most of them, categorically refused to help the Americans, insisting that his Christian beliefs forbade this as the priests had forbidden anyone to read them under pain of Hell-fire. Neither money nor presents prevailed. The old man insisted that he was so old and weak that he must soon die and he had no intention of cutting off his own road to salvation. Finally, afraid of giving way to temptation, the old man fled to the hills with the intention of staying there in hiding until the Americans had gone.

It was ,a question of the utmost importance to science. Perhaps the old man's death would remove the last chance of interpreting these mysterious *Kohau-rongo-rongo* and the Americans were ready to employ all and every means.

Just before sunset on the eve of the American's departure, heavy clouds began coming up from the south-west, an infallible sign of an approaching storm. During the subseqent downpour Thomson and some companions, including Salmon, hurried across the island from Vinapu to Mataveri where, as they had hoped, they found Ure Vaciko in his tiny hut sheltering from the storm. The old man was sleeping peacefully. When he awoke and realized that there were people all round him and escape was impossible, he fell into such a panic that not only would he not touch one of the tablets, but even refused to look at them. After much persuasion he agreed to a compromise, consenting to tell his visitors something about the old customs and traditions of the Easter Islanders. He did this surprisingly readily, perhaps because he had seldom had such a good audience. The session lasted well into the night, the Americans taking frantic notes. When almost exhausted, they produced flasks of whisky and had drinks to revive themselves. The old man watched the flask going round, then asked if he too might be allowed the "cup of consolation". After a little, the whisky did its work. The old man became quite expansive and forgot all his panic and fears.

Thomson realized that it was now or never. He tried yet another ruse, producing prints of the superb photographs of the Tahiti tablets he showed them to Ure. The old man had never seen a photograph before and could not get over his surprise. However, this was not a wooden tablet, thus the priests' prohibition did not apply, or so the old man logically told himself, and when he was told that the photographs came from the pious Bishop Jaussen, whom the priests had taught him to honour, all his lingering doubt was swept away and without further prompting he began to recite the text of the photographs. Salmon carefully noted down phonetically all the old man said and later translated this into English.

Although not understanding a word, the Americans listened intently watching how Ure turned the photographs this way and that as his eyes followed the lines of the hieroglyphs. Yet, the speed and fluency of the recitation began to make the Americans wonder. It seemed rather suspicious that the old man, whose sight was no longer good and who had few opportunities of practising reading, should be able to read off the hieroglyphs so swiftly and fluently. When he had gone through all the photographs, the Americans asked the old man to re-read parts for them, checking this against

Salmon's notes. Each time, however, what Ure recited was the same as before. He made no mistakes.

A few days later Thomson found another old man who claimed to be a relation of the last king, Maurata, and thus, being one of the royal family, to be able to read the tablets. When he was shown the photographs, he recited the same text as Ure had. Neither, however, was able to explain the meaning of the individual hieroglyphs. There was no doubt that both had been reciting from memory. On each tablet was a separate story and these the two men seemed to know by heart. They made no mistakes, so they must have known the texts individually and, perhaps, even recognized the tablets by their appearance and thus were able to identify the text recorded on them. Both explained that the significance of the individual signs had long since been forgotten.

This confirmed the supposition at which Jaussen had arrived after his work on the tablets in Tahiti.

On their return to America Thomson wrote an interesting paper on the results of the expedition which was published by the Smithsonian Institution.

XIV

AN ENGLISH EXPEDITION

The evening was hot and windless. Round the table in the living room of Percy Edmunds' little house with its roof of corrugated iron five people sat at supper: Edmunds, their host, Catharine Scoresby-Routledge, her husband, Lieut. D.R. Ritchie, RN and Captain H.J. Gillam, master of the two-masted schooner, *Mana*, which had brought them to the island early that morning of Sunday, 29th March 1914 and dropped anchor in Cook Bay.

Percy Edmunds was manager of the Chilean company formed to exploit the resources of Easter Island and his little house was some two and a half miles south of Mataveri, at the foot of the steep side of Rano Kao. It was surrounded by a small orchard, the trees in which comprised the largest plantation on the island. Percy Edmunds had been over thirty years on the island and the story he was now telling the newcomers sounded as though taken from a thriller.

The house had been built some fifty years before by the first person to exploit the island's possibilities, Bornier, whom the islanders eventually killed. One day as he was coming down a ladder one of the natives spoke to him as he reached the ground. He turned towards the man and as he did so, another hit him on the head with a stone. He was buried on the slope just above the orchard. The site was now surrounded by a low circle of stones and Edmunds pointed through the window to where it lay, visible from where they sat.

Within a day or two of the killing, a French warship arrived. Afraid of being punished if the truth became known, the islanders invented the story of Bornier's death which has so often been repeated, namely that he fell from his horse and killed himself. The deputy manager of the island also had trouble with the Easter Islanders mainly over the theft of sheep. At that time there were three or four whites living on the island and they, fed up with the continued sheep-stealing, had decided to teach the natives a lesson. Mounting their ponies, they rode down to the village. When they began firing guns the ponies took fright and ran off, so that the white men had to retreat on foot before an incensed crowd and did so to the little house, where the five now sat, and there they spent the next few months in a state of near-siege, unable to go beyond the orchard.

The previous guests to be entertained by Percy Edmunds had been shipwrecked mariners from an American ship, *El Dorado*, who had reached the island in June the previous year. *El Dorado* was on a voyage between Oregon and the Chilean ports, at a time when a hurricane blew up. She was then far out in the Pacific in search of favourable winds and had sailed straight into the path of the storm. The captain had been in whaling ships and never previously encountered anything worse. *El Dorado* had a deck cargo of 16-foot baulks of timber. When the seas became really high, the resulting movement had caused the baulks to shift. Then they had broken loose and caused such damage that the ship began to leak. In the end, she had actually broken in half and the crew had had to take to the lifeboat.

In the lifeboat were a few tins of milk and soup, a bag of biscuits and about twenty gallons of drinking water. The captain had taken his sextant with him. He had in fact gone back to his cabin for a chronometer and charts. The chronometers were already under water, so that was that, but he had managed to get a look at the chart and seen that the nearest land was Easter Island about 1000 kilometres away as the crow flies. To reach it without a chronometer and not miss it, they had first to sail north to get on to the correct parallel, thus adding another 300 kilometres to the distance.

There were eleven persons in the small 20-foot boat and thus no room to lie down. They rationed themselves to one tin of milk or soup a day, plus a tiny amount of water. Then salt water got into the fresh. Everyone suffered from thirst and the captain had to threaten to shoot anyone who tried to drink sea water.

After nine days' sailing they caught their first glimpse of the island on the horizon, but then the wind changed and it was another forty-eight hours before they managed to reach it. They landed in a state of utter exhaustion on the uninhabited northern coast. They were suffering from severe sunburn, their feet were in such state that they were unable to walk and only one of them, the most indomitable, crawled inland to where one of Edmunds' shepherds found him. Edmunds was sent for and rescued them all. He also found himself having to provide clothes for eleven men, hence, he explained, the inadequacies of his wardrobe.

That, however, was not quite the end of the story. Captain Benson (of *El Dorado*) had bought a house in the United States for which he was paying in instalments. The last instalment was due by the end of 1913 and failure to pay it would have led to loss of the whole house. To make sure that this should not happen, the captain had repaired the ship's lifeboat that had brought them to Easter Island, victualled her and set off for Mangareva, 2500 kilometres away, together with two of his crew. To help them navigate Edmunds had given them his watch and, as none had any matches, he had instructed them in the native way of making fire by rubbing two sticks together. They must have got back to civilization because Edmunds' present guests had brought with them letters, one of which was in answer to a letter he had sent with Benson.

Captain Benson wrote his own account of his adventure which was published as *Captain Benson's Own Story*. According to this he reached Mangareva after 16 days and, two days later, sailed on again for Tahiti another 1400 kilometres away, which he reached 11 days later. The British Consul there would scarcely believe it when Benson told him that he had come from Easter Island.

It was in 1910 that Mr and Mrs Scoresby-Routledge, both of whom had done a considerable amount of travelling and exploring, went to the Anthropology Department of the British Museum with a somewhat unusual question: what place or area in the Pacific would be the most desirable object for scientific exploration? There was only one answer: Easter Island; so they had spent the winter of 1910-11 working out details of an expedition to the island. As the Panama Canal was still being built, they decided to sail round South America through the Magellan Straits. Such a voyage called for a stouter craft than they were likely to find in England and so they had one built: a good solid, two-masted schooner with an auxiliary engine and fairly luxurious fittings. She was launched in May 1912 and given the Polynesian name of *Mana* which means quite a number of things including 'happiness'.

On 28th February 1913 *Mana* raised anchor and sailed from Southampton. With brief stops at Madeira, Canary Islands and Cape Verde, she reached Brazil and sailed southwards putting in at ports in the Argentine. Then she sailed through the grim, stormy Magellan Straits to Valparaiso, the starting point for more than one of the expeditions to Easter Island.

Shortly after leaving Valparaiso a member of the crew developed typhus and they had to put in at Juan Fernandez and stay in quarantine.

The last 2000 miles of the trip had been relatively uneventful, yet they all heaved a sigh of relief when they finally made their landfall on 29th March, 1914, after twenty days at sea. It was thus thirteen months since they had left England, 147 days of which had been spent at sea.

They approached the island from the south and thus what they saw was a long line of land with low gentle hills along the northern horizon. Sailing round the south-western promontory they reached Cook Bay and intended to land near the island's main village, Hanga Roa. As soon as they entered the Bay their ship was surrounded by six or seven boats filled with Easter Islanders dressed in indeterminate scraps of European clothing. Then Percy Edmunds had arrived and taken charge of them.

At this time Percy Edmunds, who was of English descent, was the only European on the island, except for the French ship's carpenter in Hanga Roa, who had married an island woman and been so completely assimilated into the island society as no longer to count as anything but an Easter Islander.

Mana remained at the island for two months, mainly because the Scoresby-Routledges wished to complete the list of materials and things, especially scientific equipment, they might need her to bring back from Chile and they also wanted her to take back their first report for London.

They began work early, more or less at dawn, that is to say about 5 a.m. and continued as long as it was light, as it was until about 5.30 p.m. During the hours of daylight they excavated and explored. At night they wrote up their notes and prepared their reports by the indifferent light of a signal lamp.

When *Mana* finally sailed, the British party moved to Edmunds' hospitable house. This comprised six rooms, three at the front and three at the back with their own entrance. The latter and the spacious attics were put at the disposal of the visitors who had already discovered that Easter Island is not the best place for camping. The Scoresby-Routledges had begun by pitching tents some hundred yards from the house, hoping thus not to impose on Edmunds' hospitality. Each evening Edmunds had taken a lantern and conducted them to their tents pitched in the picturesque vicinity of Bornier's grave, that is on the steep slope that ends in a sheer drop to the sea. At night they could hear the waves beating against the foot of the cliff and, when there was a storm, they could feel the rock quivering beneath them. Sunrise and sunset were magnificent in such wild surroundings, but they did not make up for the discomforts of wind and rain after a hard day's work.

After three and a half months at Mataveri, they transferred their work to Rano Raraku. It took them two hours to reach the volcano along a road that traversed almost the whole island. Like others in the island it was really only a path from which the worst boulders had been removed, but you could at least travel it on horseback and even in a cart.

Rano Raraku with its gentle slopes scarcely merits the term mountain or even hill. It is more like a giant swimming pool. Here it was that the French carpenter, a man called Vincent who had come from New Caledonia and taken the local name of Vare-ta, had erected the sectional metal huts that had been sent out from England. On the way all the nuts and bolts intended to hold the sections together had been stolen and how Vincent had managed to erect them was and remains a mystery.

The expedition's new base was a very picturesque spot. To their surprise they found there one well-grown tree, called the 'parasol', which did indeed provide shade. Judging by its age it must have been planted by one or other of the missionaries. Beside the camp was the majestic lip of the crater of Rano Raraku, from the top of which there was a superb view, especially at full moon with the moonlight reflected off the sea and the silent statues casting long shadows across the grass on the side of the volcano.

Easter Island is equatorial, but even so during its winter the distant Antarctic can make its presence felt. When the wind is in the south at such a time, you need to put on a sweater.

The British were now alone with the statues and the islanders. The statues remained motionless and silent, which is more than could be said of the Easter Islanders. At that time armed opposition to the activities of the Company was not infrequent. One such revolt occurred while the British were there and Mrs Scoresby-Routledge describes it in her book. To her it was comic-opera, but real enough to the islanders who could not accept the laws and customs so different to those of their ancestors that the white man wanted to impose upon them.

The Easter Islanders had always believed implicitly in

dreams and that was the cause of the trouble. On the last day of June a magnificent old woman, called Angata, came to Edmunds with two of the island's men, and told him that she had had a prophetic dream according to which Mr Merlet, the mainland director of the Easter Island Company, was no longer alive and thus the island and all·that was in it should be given back to the Easter Islanders. Angata demanded that she should be given straightaway enough cattle for the feast to honour this great event which they were to hold on the following day. A similar demand was made to the British, but they managed to buy themselves free by giving Angata some odds and ends from Mrs Scoresby-Routledge's wardrobe.

That afternoon the islanders handed Edmunds a formal declaration of war, composed in the island's Spanish. This was dated 30th June and addressed to "Senior Ema, Mataveri" and signed "Your friend, Daniel Antonio, Hangaroa."

Almost at once the islanders began to act. They forced their way into the farmyard and house, turned out Edmunds and removed some of the cattle they found there. After that everywhere about the island columns of smoke began to rise from the fires at which they were cooking and the smell of roast meat and burning huts were proof enough that the islanders were not jesting.

The kindly islanders offered the British an ox in return for the clothing they had been given, so presumably God had changed his mind about their contribution.

For the next few days there was no further news "from the front" except that Angata had had another dream in which God had told her of his pleasure that the islanders were eating meat and had informed her that before long they would be getting even more. The British were intrigued to see how during the following ten days numerous preparations for marriage began to be made. When asked the reason, the islanders explained that previous experience had taught them that after a revolt the bachelors were sent into exile in Chile, while married men and breadwinners escaped reprisals, hence this sudden rush into matrimony. The islanders seemed quite unconcerned by the fact that Edmunds, as the highest civil authority on the island, refused to accord civil marriage in the circumstances, but they just feasted and feasted.

Meanwhile the five whites on the island and the youth from Juan Fernandez, conscious of how few they were, kept wondering what the outcome of all this might be. Edmunds, who was responsible for the Company's flocks and material goods was in a most unenviable position: but none of the others felt either safe or happy, especially when it was rumoured that the rebels were in possession of firearms. Their only comfort was the news contained in some newspapers left by a passing ship that the Chilean naval training ship, *General Baquedano*, which normally visited the island every two or five years, was intending to sail there shortly.

Scoresby-Routledge, having no official position and not being involved in any way, undertook to mediate between Edmunds and the islanders about the slaughter of cattle which had assumed serious proportions, amounting to 30 animals in a single day. He went to the village where the islanders were all assembled and told them that a Chilean warship was on her way and suggesting that until her arrival they should restrict themselves to two oxen a day. The islanders just laughed and told him that according to Angata God intended the entire herd to be their property and as to Edmunds, "he was a Protestant and obviously had no God".

When Scoresby-Routledge returned to the camp empty-handed, his wife decided that it was high time she took charge: she would go and have "a woman's talk" with Angata. She took Juan, from Juan Fernandez, to interpret and rode off down to the village rather apprehensively. Everywhere lay signs of the recent feasting: bones, bits of meat and the skins of the slaughtered cattle.

Angata was seated in front of the chaplain's house surrounded by her family. She was grey-haired and elderly with very expressive eyes. Round her neck hung a medallion with a red cross on a white background. The two women greeted each other. Thereafter Angata used only her Christian name in speaking to Mrs Scoresby-Routledge, who began by offering Angata various gifts she had taken with her and also payment for some poultry Angata had sent to the camp. Angata would not accept payment on the grounds that all food comes from God and so it was not right to take payment for it. She was obviously something of a diplomat.

Mrs Scoresby-Routledge accomplished nothing and the white men came to the difficult decision that they must move camp to the other end of the island and there hang out, if they could, until the Chilean ship arrived.

On 5th August, they were woken by Edmunds with the news that the ship had come and when they got to Mataveri they found *General Baquedano* at anchor there and the four leaders of the rebellion already in chains. These, however, were soon released. The captain explained to the astonished British that the islanders had really behaved quite decently and not even killed Edmunds, as they might so easily have done. The situation was quickly eased by the distribution of a whole cargo of clothing for the islanders which had been collected by some welfare committee from all over the world.

Six months later Angata died and the rebels thus lost their spiritual leader. However, a year later, shortly after the British left the island, one of the Company's white employees was in fact killed by the islanders and his body thrown into the sea. This is, perhaps, understandable because the Company in order to make it easier to detect thefts of stock, had issued an order forbidding islanders to own sheep or cattle and this had lowered their standard of living and caused more discontent.

On 23rd August, 1914 *Mana* returned from Chile bringing news of the murders of the Austrian Archduke in Sarajevo. The situation in the island was somewhat complicated by the arrival there of two Europeans, one of them a German, who were to work on the plantation and try to start growing tobacco. Not only that but it was said that Berlin had announced that Easter Island was to be turned into a German naval base and that a small flotilla of twelve ships then on its way from China to Valparaiso would put in at the island to establish this.

When the ships anchored in Cook Bay the British prepared for a visit from the German officers, of whom they had the highest opinion. To their surprise, however, no visitors came to their archaeological base at Rano Raraku. Unlike those of *Hyena* the Germans did not seem interested in archaeology. The British began to suspect that all was not as it should be when, except for a few officers, no one came ashore and at night none of the ships showed any lights. Nevertheless they gave the Germans some letters for various destinations in Europe (which no doubt went to the bottom in the battle of the Falkland Islands). It was only when the German employee of the Company paid a visit to one of the ships and came back with the first news that war had broken out in Europe that the British understood the situation.

For a short time after the departure of the German fleet life on the island reverted to normal, but then an epidemic of dysentry broke out. It was impossible to know whether this was a memento of the Germans' visit or something that had been transmitted with the present of clothing the islanders had been given. The islanders, having no resistance, suffered considerably.

On 23rd December, 1914 another German warship, *Prinz Eitel Friedrich*, arrived at Easter Island and stayed there until the New Year.

The British archaeologists were, of course, interested in the hieroglyphs and the old Easter Island writing. The Scoresby-Routledges knew all about Thomson's efforts, but they did not believe that Ure Vaciko had necessarily been the last to know the secret of the hieroglyphs and they set about trying to find someone else who could read the tablets.

After much questioning they were told that there was one other, an old man called Tomenika, then in the leper colony on the island. To prove his assertion, the person who provided the information showed various scraps of paper torn from a Chilean notebook and supposed to have come from Tomenika. They were covered with hieroglyphs, some of them familiar to Scoresby-Routledge from the reproductions of the tablets he had studied, but others were quite new to him and that made him all the more curious. The British went straight off to the leper colony and despite the danger of infection, then considered considerable, they paid old Tomenika a visit. They found him in his garden and Tomenika recognized the bits of paper and read what was on them. One began with the words *He timo te ako-ako*, meaning "sorrow news" and he explained that this was about Jesus Christ. Seeing how surprised and bewildered his visitors were, he explained that the "words were new, but the writing old."

On their next visit to the leper the Scoresby-Routledges took Juan with them to interpret. They found the old man sitting on a blanket on the ground, his feet bare, wearing only a long linen coat and a straw hat. He had penetrating dark brown eyes and had undoubtedly been an intelligent and handsome young man. Now, unfortunately, he was senile and at times his memory failed him completely. He at once enquired if his visitors were interested in the hieroglyphs, then asked for paper and pencil. He placed the paper between his feet in front of him and taking the pencil between thumb and index finger he drew three vertical lines, to each of which he gave a name, then he filled the spaces with tiny marks and began reciting. When asked to do so more slowly so that they could write it down, he just repeated the words several times and word for word. From the length of the recitation and the paucity of the written signs it seemed obvious that the latter only served as notes to prompt his memory of the order or beginning of the verses. Try as they could, they could not get the old man to draw more than a dozen signs. He had little memory left.

At the end of the visit, by which time he was obviously tired, the old man asked his visitors to leave him pencil and paper, promising to prepare a larger text for them when they next came.

Three days later the British were shown a sheet of paper on which were five horizontal lines closely filled with hieroglyphs. Unfortunately, again he had only repeated the same dozen signs. Juan remarked rather spitefully that Tomenika was lazy, but the old man explained that the pieces of paper were too short to write the text of the tablets which were usually about a yard long. So they glued several sheets of paper together into a long strip with the lines running horizontally. Seeing this the old man avidly seized his pencil and began writing eagerly. Scoresby-Routledge did not dare take the actual paper, being afraid of infection, and only copied the signs as they were drawn.

During subsequent visits they tried to get the old man to explain some of the principles of the hieroglyphs and the meaning of some of the individual signs; but the old man's health was deteriorating rapidly and as he was now unable to get up from his bed, they could only talk to him through the door of his hut. What they did learn was that teachers of writing had been highly esteemed and respected in Easter Island society. You began by learning to draw hieroglyphs on the soft stem of a banana using a sharp shark's tooth. It was only when you knew the signs really well that you were allowed to cut them on the precious *toro-miro* (*Sophora Toromiro*). The finished tablets were hung in wicker 'quivers' from the ceilings of the houses and were tabu — no one was allowed to touch them except the initiates, that is those able to read them. At times of inter-clan strife these tablets were much-prized booty for the victors and often perished in the flames when houses or villages were set on fire in the course of the fighting.

The old man's explanations of the fundamentals of Easter Island writing were so muddled and full of contradictions that after five such meetings the Scoresby-Routledges decided that it was useless to try any further, for it was obvious that Tomenika had forgotten everything except a few hieroglyphs and verses. During their last visit, Mrs Scoresby-Routledge went outside to collect her thoughts and think out a last question or two to put to the old man and when she went back inside, old Tomenika was visibly weaker. That evening he died, probably the last person to have known the secrets of the *Kohau rongo-rongo*.

The English were on Easter Island for almost a year and a half, during which time the expedition's ship, *Mana*, made seven trips between Valparaiso and the island with supplies and letters. She left Easter Island for the last time on 18th August 1915 taking the members of the expedition with her, their work finished.

Unfortunately, owing to a wretched accident all the precious notes Mrs Scoresby-Routledge had taken were destroyed; but on her return to Britain she wrote an exceptionally interesting book of her travels round the world and to the island of which she wrote:

> In Easter Island the past is the present, it is impossible to escape from it; the inhabitants of today are less real than the men who have gone; the shadows of the departed builders still possess the land. Voluntarily or involuntarily the sojourner must hold commune with those old workers; for the whole air vibrates with a vast purpose and energy which had been and is no more. What was it? Why was it? The great works are now in ruins, of many comparatively little remains; but the impression infinitely exceeded anything which had been anticipated, and every day, as the power to see increased, brought with it a greater sense of wonder and marvel. "If we were to tell people at home these things," said our Sailing-master, after being shown the prostrate images on the great burial place of Tongariki, "they would not believe us."

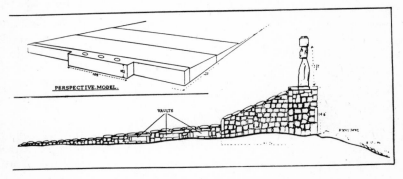

Section and perspective of the ahu platform according to Scoresby-Routledge

Thus another expedition had gathered facts which they recorded as "mysterious" and "puzzling", leaving it to others to supply the answers.

XV

A FRANCO-BELGIAN EXPEDITION

In March 1934, the latest recruit to the French navy, *Rigault-de-Genouilly*, built to maintain contact between metropolitan France and her possessions overseas, left the port of Lorient carrying in her the members of a Franco-Belgian Expedition whose destination was Easter Island. A priest blessed her from a temporary pulpit erected on the quayside, as a priest had her predecessor under the command of La Pérouse a century and a half before.

In the course of the next four months the ship put in at a number of West African and South American ports and then headed for the glaciers of Tierra del Fuego. There the expedition suffered a serious loss through the death of Charles Watelin, the famous archaeologist, who had gone out shooting in Patagonia and contracted pneumonia, so that before the ship had passed Penas Bay and reached Chile, he was dead.

The expedition had been organized to test out the theories of William Hevesy, a Hungarian scientist, who thought he saw a similarity between the hieroglyphs of *rongo-rongo* and those found in the ruined temple of Mohendzo-Daro[1] in the Indus Valley, where beneath the foundations of Buddhist buildings there had been found brick structures of the fourth millennium B.C. Research showed that these were the ruins of a large city containing numerous streets and sometimes multi-storeyed houses. Among a variety of objects found there, which proved the high state of civilization of the city, were numbers of seals of clay, stone and ivory. These seals were covered with the effigies of revered animals with hieroglyphic inscriptions which had never yet been deciphered.

Hevesy, seeing a resemblance between the two kinds of hieroglyphs, propounded far-reaching theories about the origins of the Easter Island civilization. These ideas caused quite a sensation, despite the fact that Mohendzo-Daro was

[1] It should be stressed that the Mohendzo-Daro hieroglyphs are not bustrefedon.

13,000 miles from Easter Island and thousands of years separated the two cultures, and his ideas caught on. This led another learned man, a sinologist, Heine-Geldern, to see a similarity between the Easter Island hieroglyphs and certain Chinese symbols of the Chang period.

All this, amongst other indications, led to the assumption that the main centre of civilization, if not the actual cradle of the nations of the Pacific basin, lay somewhere in Asia, whence it had spread eastwards. On that basis, people began trying to trace various sea-routes for the migrations of the peoples in the orbit of Asiatic cultures.

These theories were not confined to questions of writing, a knowledge of which among these peoples was exceptional and restricted to those at its two remotest confines: New Zealand, inhabited by the Maoris, and Easter Island. In support of these theories were arguments based on that other Easter Island mystery: its stone statues.

Because stone statues of various kinds and dimensions are to be found all over the South Pacific, it was suggested that there had at one time been an archaic megalithic civilization that had taken in the entire area from Asia to Easter Island. Proofs of this were seen in the impressive stone relics scattered at various distances from Indonesia, Micronesia to Polynesia. The gigantic triliths of the Tonga Islands, deceptively similar to the dolmens of Cornwall, were called upon as dumb witnesses to the migrations of the builders of Polynesia, to whom the erection of the giant statues on Easter Island was but a stage in their long journey which took them as far as the continent of America. The proof of their having reached it was said to be the monolithic gateway at Tiahuanaco and the palace at Cusco.

These various theories had kindled the curiosity of Paul Rivet, director of the Musée de l'Homme in Paris, who managed to get subsidies from both the French and Belgian governments to enable him to lead a scientific expedition to Easter Island. Direction of the archaeological work he entrusted to Charles Watelin and Henri Lavachery; the ethnographic and linguistic studies were under Alfred Metraux.

Each discipline had its own particular hopes. The archaeologists dreamed of finding the walls of an ancient city like Mohendzo-Daro at the foot of one or other of the volcanoes, which would answer all their questions. The ethnographers were a little more realistic: their main interest was to find the few hundred remaining Polynesians on the island who had not only survived the catastrophes of the island's history but preserved their mother tongue and retained the legends and some of the customs of their ancestors.

The expedition was joined in Lima by Henri Lavachery, formerly head conservator of the Royal Museum of Art and History in Brussels.

So, after a voyage of five months, on the morning of 27th July, 1934, they made their landfall. The gentle lines and colours of the coast reminded Dr Metraux of the pastel shades of Southern Sweden. Then the members were all summoned to the bridge where the captain told them that the seas were running so high in the vicinity of Hanga Roa, where they were hoping to land, that he could not guarantee getting their 90 packing-cases of equipment ashore and reserved the right to land them elsewhere if there was a more suitable place.

However, the ship anchored in the roads off Hanga Roa, the only village on the island that was still inhabited. Scrutiny through field-glasses of the coast and village, despite the rain, showed its Polynesian character to be undoubted.

The wind was squally and the weather obviously deteriorating to the growing disquiet of the members of the expedition. A crowd had begun to gather on the shore, but for a long time no one, it seemed, thought of putting out a boat and coming to the ship. This seemed to augur badly for the chances of their equipment being landed. Then, however, they breathed a sigh of relief as they saw first one, then a second and a third boat put out from the jetty. As they drew nearer, they saw that in the stern of the first sat the island's governor in person. It was rowed by islanders in Chilean naval uniform, whose rowing would have earned them a place in any regatta. The other two boats presented a very different picture. They were loaded almost to the gunwales with tightly-packed islanders dressed in the oddest assortment of European clothing. The only trace of local folklore was their strange headdresses ornamented with feathers, but these too were just part of a masquerade for the benefit of the visitors.

Dr Metraux who had promised himself so much from contact with the islanders felt profoundly disappointed as he observed all this from the deck of the ship. What percentage was there of the autochtones in these people, he wondered, and how much mixed blood? His anthropologist's eye scrutinized the faces of the noisy throng in the boats and he was at once struck by the number whose complexion was surprisingly pale and whose features were almost European. Then his eye was caught by the extra long nose of the steersman which reminded him of the profiles of the stone statues of which he had studied many a photograph. Next his attention was caught by the chin and low forehead of a youth, both possible signs of Polynesian origin, as might be the soft, joyful gesticulations. The islanders called out from the boats, addressing those in the newly arrived ship in English, French and Spanish: "Soap, soap, Captain, Lieutenant, soap." "Two pieces of soap for my little statue." "Your soap is small. The Chileans' is bigger. Give me another piece. Remember me, when you come ashore. I have a good horse. I'll take you to the volcano".

As he watched, Dr Metraux's sense of disappointment grew. Meanwhile, on deck the islanders displayed the goods they wished to barter: trash, the lot of it: crude carvings, statuettes, sticks — inept copies of the wonderful works of art produced by their ancestors. This was almost mass production, aimed at appealing to the ordinary seaman and obtaining a cake of soap, a pair of pants or any article of European clothing. They had learned all too swiftly from the island's exploiters.

A young good-looking islander came up to Dr Metraux, introduced himself as Pedro Atan and asked what the purpose of the expedition was. When Metraux told him that they had come to look for archaeological specimens, the youth nodded understandingly and told the doctor that there were very few old things left and any search for them would be long and protracted; but, he added, that was a difficulty that could be overcome. The islanders would make as many of whatever kind of antiquity the expedition required and nobody would know the difference or be any the wiser. The doctor and the other members of the expedition were horrified by the implications of such a proposition, which, to say the least of it, was a warning not to buy specimens from the islanders.

Dr Metraux now had to go and greet the island's governor, who was just coming aboard. His official title was *subdelegado* and for the occasion he wore a splendid uniform. No sooner had they exchanged greetings than the governor was informed of their difficulties over landing the equipment. He promised to organize help and invited the new arrivals to come ashore in his boat. No sooner in the boat, than they realized why the ship's captain had felt so doubtful about being able to land their packing-cases. For several minutes the boat they were in was tossed up and down like a cork and they only got into calmer water when they reached the shelter of the breakwater. As they were being rowed along the inside the breakwater, they examined it and its structure with interest: there was no doubt, it had been built of stone from the ruined *ahu* and perhaps other ancient structures on the island.

Willing, helping hands hauled them up onto the breakwater and there they stood, not quite knowing what to do. They could scarcely believe that they were in Polynesia, so different was it to what they had imagined.

The sky was overcast and from the lowering clouds fell a steady drizzle. In an instant they found themselves surrounded by a throng of inquisitive men, women and children, all clamouring in English and Spanish. The women they thought ugly in their damp, shapeless garments that they wore without any grace or elegance. Then a youngish woman approached one of them and asked for a cigarette. When he proferred a packet for her to take one, she snatched the whole packet and ran off as fast as she could. This broke the slight awkwardness of the situation, but also was a vivid reminder of the account by previous expeditions of the chronic lightfingeredness of the islanders. This incident was a second warning.

As they were walking away from the breakwater, they saw coming towards them the short, bowed figure of an old man with grey hair dressed in clothes that were obviously too big for him. Holding out a wrinkled, coloured hand the old man greeted them in French: "*Bonjour, Messieurs!*" It was indeed Vincent Poro, a fellow countryman of whom they had read in the reports of other expeditions. He was the French ship's carpenter who had settled in Easter Island sixty years before, married an island girl and was now the head of a numerous family. Although he had let himself be absorbed completely into island society, Poro had never taken any interest in their customs and so was of little use to the expedition, at any rate as a source of information.

The members of the expedition first went to the *subdelagacion*, which was both the office and the home of the island's governor. They walked along surrounded by a throng of islanders and Dr Metraux was astounded to see that the prettiest girl he had observed there so far, in an attempt to make herself more pleasing, had covered her face with powdered rice so that it was white all over.

Near the *subdelagacion* they were met by two white men, Morrison and Smith, representatives of the firm of Williamson, Balfour and Co. which owned the herds of cattle and flocks of sheep on the island. Morrison and Smith invited the newcomers to make their quarters at the Company's farm in Mataveri and this the newcomers were glad to accept, realizing that it was the best way of ensuring their comfort and safety.

By the entrance to the *subdelagacion* stood a good-looking young woman with a baby in her arms. She was the governor's wife and appeared to be quite unmoved by having her house invaded by a horde of soaking men. Inside they met an amusing character; he had fat cheeks, was unshaven and dressed in rather gaudy pyjamas and slippers. He introduced himself as a bankrupt Chilean business man who had taken refuge in the island, where he acted as teacher and public letter-writer. During the months they spent on the island the members of the expedition met the man on several occasions and always he was unshaven and dressed in the same way.

It never stopped raining all that day. Soaked to the skin and depressed by the difficulties of unloading their equipment, the newcomers felt less and less inclined to believe that there was any romance about Easter Island. A little more genuine Polynesian atmosphere was provided by the arrival of Victoria Rapahango — on horseback. Dressed all in white, with beautiful ringlets of dark hair falling over her shoulders, she made a very pleasing impression that was only enhanced by the friendship that grew up between them all. A member of the royal family, she was then thirty-six. Her irreproachable manners, pride and poise, plus her intelligence and sense of humour, made her a very welcome change to the other islanders.

After a short pause, the rain came pouring down harder than ever, blotting out everything but a short stretch of the beach on which the scientists stood watching their baggage being unloaded. One after the other the packing-cases were dumped down in the midst of a crowd of gawping spectators who refused to be deterred by rain, wind or anything. This made the scientists more and more apprehensive. All the white men on the island they had met had warned them about the thieving propensities of the islanders, and the latter's effusive assurance of their honesty and desire to help did nothing to set their minds at rest, so there they stayed guarding their things and supervising the unloading. Every now and then a woman would step out of the throng of spectators and coming up to the white men ask rather pointedly if they did not by chance have a cake of soap or, better still, a bottle of scent for her.

It was evening and already dark before the unloading was complete. Late though it was, they decided to go straight to Mataveri. The steep path was fringed by a low wall of undressed stones and lined with mulberry trees. At first the prosaic European aspect irritated them, but later they grew to love it.

Just before they reached the level at Mataveri, a shadow detached itself from the darkness, came up to Dr Metraux, thrust a handful of stone objects into his hand, said: "Regala — this is a present from me," and vanished. The stone proved to be obsidian spear heads and made the first present the expedition had had on the island. As it proved, to the end of their stay they were to be unable to become quits. The spearheads were the start of a vicious circle of gift and return of gift, local custom requiring that each present be requited with another. But of that they were still blissfully unaware and felt that the present augured well.

Finally they reached the farm which was set in a grove of well-grown eucalyptus trees that was almost unique in the island and there they were hospitably received by Mrs Smith. They soon saw that the farm and the rest of the island were two different worlds. They were intrigued and wanted to investigate the relations of the Company and the islanders. What they had heard about the Company while in Chile had not been too complimentary and had included charges of brutality and that the islanders were no longer allowed to move freely about the lands of their ancestors, but more or less confined to Hanga Roa. There had been talk of economic exploitation and starvation wages. Dr Metraux ventured to ask their host about this and was told that the Company's employees received four pesos and a portion of meat every day and that the Company considered this adequate and that it was better than that of the ordinary *peon* in Chile itself. During the sheep-shearing there was work for the women and children as well and they were paid piece rates. Dr Metraux then told Smith what they had heard in Chile about the inordinate profits made by the Company on the goods it sold to the islanders. Smith was highly indignant and replied that the actual fact was that they sold at wholesale prices despite the high costs of transport. He insisted that some of their prices were lower than those in Chile as was proved by the fact that the crews of the Chilean ships often bought supplies on the island before they left. He was well aware that the islanders complained of the disproportion between their earnings and the price of goods, but that was not the Company's fault, but that of the economic crisis in Chile.

Smith's guests found these explanations not altogether convincing. Next they asked why the islanders were all concentrated in the small area of Hanga Roa and were told that though the island formally belonged to Chile it was the property of the company, Williamson and Balfour, which ran sheep on it and bred cattle and pigs on a smaller scale. The island's climate and grass were excellent for sheep, which bred well and gave a good crop of wool. At that time they had 40,000 on the island. These should have been easy to tend, but the islanders were inveterate thieves. They had eaten all the sheep the missionaries had reared and would do the same with the Company's, if it did not take preventative measures. These included isolating the native village from the rest of the island with barbed wire and the use of native police recruited from the most honest and loyal elements. After sunset no one was allowed to cross the wire without a special pass. In fact two days before the ship's arrival, the farm had been broken into and all the lambs in it taken. They knew the culprits, but that was no help as no one had been caught red-handed. All the native police were close or distant relatives of the culprits and would give no one away, let alone arrest them. If in such a case, they had complained to the governor, he would have feigned indignation, promised to punish the guilty and — done nothing more. In fact, the governor was delighted over the Company's difficulties and not prepared to do anything to end them. The islanders were inveterate rogues. At the beginning of the year, they had broken into the store and plundered it so thoroughly that at the present time they had neither sugar, tobacco or soap and the next ship was not due for six months. Every child in the island knew who had robbed the store, but how were they to be punished? The Company had no proof and knew that in court those who had given information, would swear that they knew nothing and had said nothing. This time even the governor was feeling the effects, because he needed things from the Company's store as much as anyone. Even so, for all his promises, he never got round to doing anything.

What the Company disliked most, Smith went on, was not

so much the islanders' attitude, but their hypocrisy. Chile was quite indifferent and took no interest in the island and the islanders. The Company only wanted to look after its own interests and tried to be humane and all the thanks it got was to be accused of abusing the islanders.

The next morning Metraux and his companions went to Hanga Roa. All the islanders they met on the way there greeted them with the Tahitian greeting: *ia-o-rana*. They also met groups of sailors on their way to Mangareva accompanied by laden porters hired for a shirt or a cake of soap.

Not far from the landing place they made the acquaintance of the person who for the next five months was to be their main intermediary between the present and the island's past, their oracle and main source of information about the island and its people. This was Juan Tepano. The scientists were struck even at this first encounter by his individuality. He was sitting on a slab of rock by the roadside with a woollen cap on his head and a pipe in his mouth and seemed to be the typical sharp-witted hero of romantic novels. There was nothing Polynesian about his features. In fact he looked much more like a Paris Bohemian and to some extent that was how he regarded himself, as he considered himself a highly talented sculptor. His work was original and beautiful, though quite different from the traditional art of the island. His fame had in fact spread to the mainland and Metraux and his companions already knew of him as an authority on ethnographical matters. Tepano was obviously flattered by their mention of this and rather fulsomely said to them:

"Your expedition shall learn everything about the island and its past. Those who were here before you were unable to understand words, but these shall all be confided to you. I know that the words of my ancestors have been twisted, but you shall be given them unchanged."

As they looked at him Metraux and his companions wondered about his age: he looked young and this and his brisk movements seemed to belie what they had been told of his advanced years. Records had only just been started to be kept on the island, so there was no means of checking his age. When asked about it, he told them that he was not less than eighty. Later they were to discover that he was only about sixty. At this first meeting, however, he obviously wanted to make himself out as very, very old — as old as the last builders of statues.

Tepano then asked his new acquaintances to his home and

they walked there along an avenue of mulberries that led into a tiny square with wooden benches in front of a church. Most of the houses in the village were built of wood and had corrugated iron roofs. Everywhere, in every alleyway were the ordinary signs of poverty. It was a village that could have been anywhere in Chile. Tepano's home, however, was built of undressed stone "like those of our ancestors" as he proudly informed them as he ushered them inside. When they had got to know him better, the members of the expedition decided that he lived in a stone hut because he was too lazy to stir himself to get the planks for a wooden house.

There were two rooms. The first was furnished with two iron bedsteads and a rickety table. The other room was a little more exotic: a fire burned on the floor in the middle of it and round it some women were busied preparing a meal in iron pots. In a far, dark corner they saw a strange squatting figure that seemed to be all wrinkles. It was seated on a bundle of straw and held out five talon-like fingers towards the visitors. This was Viriamo, Tepano's mother, who had been born "in the days of our kings" and was now in her second childhood. Her son presented her to the visitors as if she had been an exhibit in a museum. He told them that when the first missionaries came to the island in 1864, Viriamo was already married. He made the visitors admire the tattooing on her feet, assuring them that when she was young, she had been able to talk with the devil. It was to his mother, he said, that he owed most of his knowledge of the island's past and of the ancient customs of its people. If only the expedition had gone there twenty years earlier, Metraux thought, she would have been able to tell them so much.

The news of the visitors' arrival in the village had even assembled a throng outside Tepano's house and when they emerged Metraux and the others were showered with questions. They decided that this was the appropriate moment to announce their intention to pay with an article of clothing for any genuine and worthwhile relic of the past that was brought to them. And the announcement produced results.

That evening a woman, looking very secretive, slipped a stone fish hook into Metraux's hand and demanded due payment. It was not until after payment had been made that they discovered the hook to be a fake. This was yet another object lesson to the expedition, which was to have ample opportunity to discover how highly developed among the islanders was the art of faking antiquities. Not only were the things the islanders made faithful copies of the originals, but they were able to coat them with a patina that made if difficult indeed to tell the new from the old. Indeed, Metraux deliberately bought copies of some objects, original examples of which were not to be had, because they were so perfect.

A few days after engaging Tepano as their guide, Metraux and his companions went to the *ahu* Tupru with Tepano and some members of his family and there pitched camp. Thus began the laborious work of excavation and exploration that was to continue for more than five months. The expedition covered the whole of the island, bivouacking wherever there were relics of the past to be examined. While Lavachery measured and investigated ruins, Metraux made notes of the legends and traditions connected with the place from Tepano's dictation.

The expedition spent the last two months of its stay near Hanga Roa, completing their collection of ethnographical material. Being near the village, Dr Drapkin spent his time helping the islanders who remembered him with gratitude for many a long day.

The planned period of five months soon passed and around the New Year the Belgian training ship *Mercator* anchored in the roads off Hanga Roa and on 2nd January, 1935, the expedition left the island.

XVI

THE DESCENDANTS OF MAKLAJ

One day in the summer of 1940 the pupils of Class 10 of School 147 in Leningrad were taken to the Great Museum of Anthropology and Ethnography in their city. On the third floor, where were the collections of the famous Russian traveller Mikolay Miklucho-Maklaj, three of the boys, Borys Kudriawcew, Valery Czernuskow and Oleg Klitin, found themselves fascinated by the two wooden tablets from Easter Island, one of which Miklucho-Maklaj had been given by Bishop Jaussen. One tablet was shaped like a knife, the other was rather like a boomerang and both were covered with hieroglyphs, and the fact that no one knew what the hieroglyphs meant fired their imagination and they decided to try to find out for themselves.

They became so interested that they formed their own little society which they called "Descendents of Maklaj" and their declared purpose was to decipher the Easter Island tablets — no less! The three young boys set about the task seriously and most systematically, starting with a study of all available literature. They were obviously so keen that the museum authorities did everything they could to help them.

The tablets were described thus by the famous Miklucho-Maklaj:

Both sides of the plank are covered with these hieroglyphs. They are arranged in horizontal rows. There are no spaces between the verses and the entire surface of the tablet is covered with hieroglyphs: every hollow, inequality and all the edges have been carved. The verses are distinguished in an original manner: when you get to the end of one, you have to turn the tablet the other way up to read the next. This is easily seen from the heads of the different figures. The hieroglyphs have been carved or stamped out with a sharp instrument. Many of them depict animals. Many of the symbols are repeated over and over again, the figure being unchanged or changed in one particular (head or hand turned in a different direction, or hand holding something etc.). Sometimes two figures are joined together, sometimes three or even more are joined. Looking at the lines of these hieroglyphs, you cannot help feeling that here you are dealing with the lowest stage in the development of writing, called pictorial writing.

Having to turn the tablet the other way up so frequently meant that reading these long tablets was an inconvenient and uncomfortable business, so the three young men set about copying the different signs. At first they used the earlier method of comparing the drawings in an attempt to systematize them and arrive at a sort of alphabet. This was no easy task as one tablet had 728 signs on it and the other 1171.

Then the three had an original idea: instead of comparing the individual signs, they would compare the two tablets, which no one had yet thought of doing. They began by redrawing the signs on both tablets in the order in which they had been carved with one text under the other, that is to say the first hieroglyphs on the 'knife' tablet beneath the first on the 'boomerang' tablet and so on. This led to the startling discovery that certain groups were repeated on both tablets, and even more extraordinary, that the two texts were identical. The tablets or copies of them had already been in the hands of scholars all over the world, yet no one had noticed that they were identical.

The three then decided to use their method on the other tablets elsewhere in the world and these they first had to track down. In the end, it appeared that in all only twenty-five had survived: apart from the two in Leningrad, there were nine in the Belgian museum at Braine-le-Comte, near Brussels, two in the capital of Chile, Santiago; the others in the British Museum.

There was, of course, no book or publication with adequate reproductions of them all and, this being wartime, it was not possible to send everywhere for photographs of them. They began searching through the books in the secondhand and antiquarian bookshops of Leningrad and in the end found themselves with adequate reproductions of two further tablets: of that in Santiago Museum and of one of those in Braine-le-Comte.

They were now able to compare four tablets instead of just two. Again they found that all four texts were identical.

The work of the three had now attracted the attention of Russian scholars and Professor Olderogge proposed to Borys Kudriawscew that they should collaborate. However, once

only sandy beach on the island and that made the landing of stores and equipment very much easier. Also it was the place where legend says Hotu-matua first stepped ashore.

When the members of the expedition returned from visiting the island's governor, Arnoldo Curti, Heyerdahl found the ship's company in a state of consternation because, when some islanders had come aboard, the captain had produced the ship's visitors' book for them to sign, but no one would do so and the captain unable to believe that they were unable to write, had asked the Chilean archaeologist who could speak Spanish with the islanders, to get their autographs. The request had caused quite an uproar. Eventually it transpired that the reason for all this was the memory of the trick played on the islanders in 1862 by a Chilean flotilla of seven ships. When the islanders had swarmed aboard those ships they had delightedly taken the opportunity to scribble with pencils on sheets of paper set before them, quite unaware that by doing so they were "putting their mark" to a contract binding them to mine guano on the islands off the coast of Peru. When they had wanted to go ashore, they had been prevented by force and taken off into slavery, leaving almost no one in the island.

Next day, when the expedition went ashore at Anakena, they had no sooner landed than over the crest of the rise came a solitary horseman. This proved to be the local herdsman, in charge of the sheep in that part of the island, who lived in a little hut of whitewashed stone on the western side of the "Valley of the Kings". When he heard that they were intending to make camp in the valley there, he pointed out a narrow gorge in which were numerous caves, where, he said, the island's first king, Hotumatua, had lived with his suite when they first landed, before they had built themselves roomier houses of reeds.

He spoke of the king with the complete assurance of one relating well-established fact. Then hearing that the expedition had its own waterproof tents and did not need caves, he suggested that these be pitched on the other side of the beach, where Hotumatua's house used to stand. This was a terrace at the foot of a low, rounded hill.

All round was evidence of the island's splendid past: big stone *ahu* and numerous toppled, grey stone statues, behind one of which the herdsman reverently pointed to the remains of the foundations of the king's "palace".

The place seemed a good one and there they pitched their tents.

A couple of days later they began digging. This revealed the pentagonal stove of the royal kitchens and near it a stone foundation in the shape of a boat.

Just below the turf they found pieces of a stone bowl, spear heads and some sharp instruments of black volcanic glass. Lower down they found fish hooks of human bone and of stone. At the depth of about one foot they came across another pentagonal stove, identical to the first. Examining this they found the charred remains of fish hooks, shells, human bones and teeth. Deeper still they found a pretty blue bead, of a kind used in Europe for trade with the Indians two hundred years before. Roggeveen's journal mentions how among the presents given to the islanders who came aboard were two strings of blue beads, and evidently one of these found its way to the royal premises in Anakena. Thus the date of the second stove was the period of the first European visits to the island.

Though modest, the results of these preliminary excavations aroused great hopes. There was no doubt in the minds of Heyerdahl and his companions that archaeological excavation was essential, and so with the help of the governor and Father Sebastian he engaged workmen and after a scientific reconnaissance they set about systematic digging in various parts of the island.

Dr William Mulloy, of the University of Wyoming, and twenty men spent four months on the most famous sacred place on the island — the platform *ahu* in Vitapu. This was the site favoured by Heyerdahl who in the stonework of the *ahu* saw similarities with the pre-Inca walls of Peru. After parts of the *ahu* had been uncovered, it appeared that the building had been re-built and lengthened several times by architects who were successively worse at their job. The older the piece, the better the technique, a fact that seemed to contradict the theory of gradual development and perfection of stoneworking in the island; indeed it showed that the earliest buildings had been put up by people with an excellent knowledge of their craft and that later this craft had deteriorated. The other American archaeologists, Edwin Ferdon and Carlyle Smith, working on other *ahu* independently reached the same conclusion.

This led Heyerdahl to state that there were three distinct epochs in the history of Easter Island: first a people of a highly developed culture employing the typical building techniques of the Incas, huge blocks of hard basalt cut like cheese and fitted together without any gap. Then, in the second epoch, most of the classical buildings were partially dismantled and rebuilt and in front of them concave, paved platforms were built; huge statues were brought from Rano Raraku and set up on the tops of these rebuilt walls. At the height of this activity, the work was brought to a sudden, unexpected standstill, after which the island was given over to war and cannibalism — that being the last, tragic phase of the history of the mysterious island. No one any longer knew how to dress stone; the standing statues were overthrown indiscriminately. Round stones and shapeless blocks were built into funeral mounds along the walls of the *ahu*, often using the overthrown statues as natural roofs for their burial chambers. In this phase there is no sign of plan or professional knowledge. The technique of the Incas was brought to the island when fully developed and brought by a civilized people who themselves were not indigenous.

This was only the start. One day Mulloy uncovered a red stone so unusual that he sent for Heyerdahl. Did Heyerdahl agree, he asked, that on the stone was a hand with fingers? The red stone was long, like a rectangular pillar, though as yet only one side was exposed. Heyerdahl at once recognised a great similarity to the red columnar figures he had seen in the Andes, which were of pre-Inca origin. Closer examination removed any doubt that the five marks were fingers. Apart from them, however, there was no other sign whether of head or other human features. The stone was unlike any other in the island both in shape and material. It had not come from the quarries at Rano Raraku. At the sight of it the islanders just shrugged and pronounced it an ordinary *hani-hani* red stone.

Heyerdahl, who remembered having seen such rectangular columns on the shores of Lake Titicaca, told them to continue digging. As they cleared the earth away round the column, first a forearm, then an arm, a whole hand — and then a second came to light. The figure was of a type hitherto unknown on Easter Island. The head unfortunately had been knocked off and a deep hole had been drilled where the heart should be. It also had short legs.

Further discoveries followed, more stone figures of a type never before seen on the island and not even mentioned in the verbal traditions of the islanders who gazed at them in amazement.

The general academic view was that the first inhabitants of Easter Island had come there from the West, from Central

Polynesia, in a succession of waves between the twelfth and sixteenth centuries AD. This view was based mainly on analysis of local information. According to the chronology of the legendary kings of the island, the supposed date of the arrival there of Hotumatua seemed to be AD 1150. However, using carbon-dating on a dozen organic objects they dug up Dr Smith was able to date the oldest find at about AD 380, thus showing that the history of the island must be at least 800 years older than had been supposed. This date was arrived at independently in the laboratories of three countries and is the oldest date so far recorded in Polynesia.

Heyerdahl's opponents had hitherto countered his argument by pointing to the so-called chronological barrier: how could there have been links between America and Polynesia, when on the continent the Indian peoples had achieved a high level of craftsmanship in stone and were expert astronomers, while on the islands of the Pacific they had scarcely begun to learn such things? Heyerdahl's discoveries now provided the missing links in the chain and destroyed the chronological barrier.

One of the most interesting objects excavated was a large statue, quite different from the usual bust-statues. This figure had a lower part and legs. It was carved in a kneeling posture, buttocks resting on its heels and hands placed on its knees. Unlike the others, it was not naked, but wearing a poncho with a square opening for the head, which was unusual in being rounded, bearded and in having protruding eyes. The expression of the face was itself quite different from that of any others found on Easter Island.

The islanders had never seen anything like it, but to both Gonzalo and Heyerdahl it was familiar, for in Tiahuanaco, the oldest centre of the pre-Inca civilization, both had seen similar kneeling stone giants which might easily have been carved by the same hand, so similar in conception were they.

Edwin Ferdon, digging at the village of the man-birds, made discoveries of great interest. He dismantled a small, ill-built *ahu* to find that it had been built on the ruins of a much older structure of enormous well-fitted blocks made with the Inca technique. Further digging revealed round sun symbols, so common in South America, carved on the stone. Among the symbols was a system of holes bored in the rock. Their symmetry and similarity to ones he had seen in Latin America suggested that here was a ritual astronomical observatory. The summer solstice of the southern hemisphere falls on 21st December, then only a few days away. On that date Ferdon and the ship's captain went to the site, Ferdon stuck a stick in one of the holes and as the sun rose above the lip of the crater, the black shadow of the stick fell on the opening Ferdon had previously marked. This experiment was repeated at the next two solstices with the same result. There was no doubt: they had found the first and so far the only astronomical observatory of Polynesia.

Dr Mulloy made a similar interesting discovery when he took his measuring instruments to the big *ahu* excavated at Vinapu at the summer solstice. His instruments showed that the sun's rays fell vertically on to the great wall built with the Inca technique. It was beside this *ahu* that the first crematorium in the island was found. Here many people had been burned and buried, some with fishing equipment.

Like the members of all previous expeditions, Heyerdahl and his associates could not imagine how the islanders had been able to transport and erect these huge stone statues, some of which had been taken ten miles from the quarry. What was perhaps stranger was that the colossal statues had not been transported to the site as rough blocks which would not have suffered damage, but ready carved and finished except for the eyes, in which state they were easily damaged. Once they had been erected the masons carved out their eyes. This still left the most difficult task of all: capping the statue with the huge red 'hat' which weighed anything from two to ten tons.

Heyerdahl thought the term 'hat' used by previous investigators inaccurate. The islanders' word for them was *pukao*, meaning hair-dress, in effect that of the islanders at the time of the island's discovery. These ancient sculptors had not carved any hair, but placed it on top, because they were concerned with the colour, its red, which may perhaps have had some connection with fairly general red-hairedness of the original inhabitants. Usually, there were two statues on each *ahu*, yet on many there were four, five or six, and on one platform as many as fifteen in a row on a walled base that was four metres high.

Today none of the statues stand where they were put. Probably at the time of the island's discovery by the Dutch most of the statues had already been toppled from the platforms. The last were overthrown during the cannibal strife of about 1840. This was thirty feet high and had a red 'hat' of six cubic metres. Its base was as high as a man. Weighing fifty tons, it had been brought from the quarry at Rano Raraku nearly three miles away. Having been got there, the statue was winched up on to its tall base and set upright and then its head, four-storeys up as it were, topped with a hair-dress weighing ten tons. This hair-dress had had to be brought seven miles from where it was quarried, a task that appears as nothing compared with that of hoisting it into place thirty feet up.

Father Sebastian counted over 600 stone statues in the island. On one side of the crater of Rano Raraku is a huge cut, like a slice cut from a giant cake, made by the island's masons. Heyerdahl estimated that more than 20,000 cubic metres of stone had been taken from there and the archaeologists reckoned that one would be justified in doubling the figure.

In an attempt to solve the mystery of the means used to quarry, carve, transport and erect these statues, Heyerdahl, after consulting Father Sebastian, decided to commission a statue from the islanders, as one would order a suit from a tailor. The 'order', they decided, must be given to genuine descendents of the old masons, that is to the greatgrandchildren of Ororoina the only survivor of the massacre of the long-eared.

According to Father Sebastian there were only eighteen or nineteen people in the whole island who could be said to be of pure blood and only one family descended directly from Ororoina. When adopting Christianity at the end of the last century this family had taken the name Adam (or Atan as the islanders pronounced it) and the eldest of the brothers Atan was Pedro Atan, the headman.

Atan, proud of his descent, accepted the order as if it was a question of making a few crude *kava-kava* figures that were produced en masse for the tourists and not a huge statue several yards high. Equally surprising to Heyerdahl was the obvious knowledge with which Atan set to work. Having been told that the statue was to be of medium size, that is about sixteen feet high, he said that six people would be needed for a statue of that size. There were only four Atans, but there were others related to the long-eared on their mother's side whom he could co-opt. Next Heyerdahl applied to the island's governor for permission to quarry stone at Rano Raraku and for Pedro Atan to be temporarily relieved of his civic duties.

The day before work was to begin Pedro Atan asked Heyerdahl to honour the old tradition by preparing food for the masons. When, by nightfall, no one had come for it,

Heyerdahl and his companions went to bed. About midnight they heard singing and a strange humming, accompanied by rhythmical trampling on the grass-grown earth. Looking out, Heyerdahl was surprised to see in the space in the middle of the camp a group of squatting figures beating on the ground with carved clubs, the sticks used in their dances and stone axes. All of them were wearing crowns of feathery leaves and the smaller figures on either fringe wore paper masks of men-birds with huge eyes and great beaks. Those on the fringe swayed backwards and forward while the others rocked this way and that, singing and beating time on the ground. The melody they sang had an almost hypnotic effect: it sounded like a greeting from a vanished world; yet Heyerdahl thought he had heard the same sort of tune in an Indian pueblo in New Mexico and on this point his archaeologists agreed.

At the end of the ceremony Heyerdahl presented the dancers with a dish of meat the steward had previously cooked, and after a while Pedro Atan brought it back empty. He was grave and serious and explained that this was an ancient ceremony and the song that which the sculptors and masons had always sung, which they did in honour of their most important god, Atua, asking that they might succeed in the enterprise on which they were embarking.

The masons spent the night in one of the nearby caves of Hotumatua. Then early the next morning they all set out for the quarry at Rano Raraku. Here the masons began collecting the old stone axes, of which literally hundreds littered the terraces. These axes were conical and looked like claws.

Having selected the rock face they wanted, the islanders made piles of these old axes at the foot of it, and each of the team set a gourd full of water beside him. Although none of them were masons by trade and this was undoubtedly the first time in their lives they had undertaken such a commission, they all seemed to know exactly what to do and how to do it.

Pedro Atan, still wearing his ceremonial wreath, was everywhere checking that all was in order. Then he began measuring using his open arm or his fingers, marking the rock face with his stone axe. This finished, he asked for them all to be excused and they withdrew behind a projection to perform some secret ritual. Returning, they lined up facing the measured rock, axe in hand, held like a dagger. At a sign from Pedro, they began singing the song sung the previous evening and at the same time in unison raising their arms and stabbing at the rock with their axes. They quickly warmed to the task, while Heyerdahl and the others watched as though hypnotized. They sang and sang, striking the rock in time with the song. Perhaps this was the first time for a hundred years that Rano Raraku had resounded to the sound of axes. One blow did not have much effect, beyond dislodging a little dust, but as blow followed blow things began to happen. Every so often the masons sprinkled a little water on the place they were striking.

This went on all the first day and throughout the second and third days. At the end of which the outline of the statue was clearly visible. They cut two parallel perpendicular grooves, then chipped away the rock in between. They kept changing axes, picking up another when one blunted. Formerly it had been thought that the axes were discarded when they became blunted, hence the great number littering the ground; but this proved to be false. When Pedro's axe blunted, he struck it against another axe lying on the ground sending slivers of stone flying and in no time at all he had a sharp axe. It was like sharpening a pencil.

It looked then as if the axes lying everywhere had been in use simultaneously, each mason having a considerable number that he used alternately. Not many masons were employed on each figure. The average sixteen-foot statue required six masons: and several hundred must have been needed to produce that great number of statues. In some cases, one could see that work on a statue had been halted for technical reasons before even the quarry had been abandoned. Either the rock had split; or they had run into flint on which their axes could make no impression.

At the end of three days, the team came to Heyerdahl and showed him their hands covered with blisters, lamenting that though used to working all day, this *moai* or mason's work was unaccustomed and they could not maintain the same tempo as their ancestors week after week. Naturally, Heyerdahl agreed to their interrupting their labours. From his point of view, the experiment had been completely successful: he now knew the technique of the masons, which previously no one had been willing to reveal, or perhaps the great majority of the islanders had no knowledge of it.

On the basis of what they had accomplished in three days, Heyerdahl was able to calculate the amount of time required to cut one figure completely. Mrs Scoresby-Routledge had estimated that it had taken fifteen days; and Alfred Metraux, though thinking fifteen days too little, had also underestimated the time. Both had under-estimated the hardness of the stone. Pedro Atan reckoned that working all day in two shifts it would take a year to cut one statue. His relatives thought that it would take fifteen months. Dr Mulloy working it out scientifically arrived at the same figure, one year.

Delighted with the result of this first experiment, Heyerdahl wished to continue, so, one day when Pedro was in a good mood, he suggested that he and the team should try using the methods of their ancestors to raise one of the recumbent statues and set it up again on its base. Pedro agreed to this, saying that he needed money to go to Chile. A fee of 100 dollars was agreed.

Some days later Pedro and eleven of the descendents of the long-eared ones appeared in the valley of the kings and took up quarters in Hotumatua's cave. Just before nightfall that day he appeared in the camp where in silence he dug a smallish hole in the space between the tents and disappeared.

Later that night, the occupants of the camp heard the distant strains of an unfamiliar melody and dull drumming, similar to the sounds of the night before work began in the quarry. Now, however, both the ceremony and the melody were different. Pedro's brother went and stood on a stone that had been placed in the hole Pedro had dug, and on the stone he beat time, stamping his feet.

The next morning the twelve got to work. The statue they were going to raise was the largest of those lying in the valley and weighed between 25 and 30 tons, thus to raise it each would have had to lift more than two tons. Nonetheless, the team went about their preparations as quietly and with as much assurance as if they had never done anything else. Their only tools were three round poles (latterly reduced to two) which they used as levers and various stones chosen from the many lying all round. Though the island is now treeless except for a few plantations of eucalyptus, trees have always grown round the lake in the crater at Rano Karaku, where the first visitors to the island found a grove of *toro miro* which is a kind of hibiscus. Thus the three poles seemed permissible tools. The statue's face was deep in the ground, so the ends of the poles had to be dug in. That done, several hung on to the end of each pole, while Pedro lying on his belly inserted stones under the head. Sometimes the members of the expedition, who were watching, could see a slight movement in the stone, but usually there was nothing to be seen, but Pedro inserting stone after stone. As the hours passed, he was selecting bigger and bigger stones, and by evening, the statue's head was a good three feet above ground, resting on a pile of stones. The following day, they discarded one of the poles as no longer being necessary. This left five on each of the remaining two poles. Pedro put his youngest brother to insert the stones under the statue and himself stood on the wall with his arms raised like someone conducting an orchestra, and as he beat time, he called out: "*Etahi, erua, etoru!* One, two, three! One, two, three! Hold, Stone." Then began again: "One, two, three! One, two, three! Hold, Stone!"

Slowly, but steadily the statue rose as the heap of stones grew and grew. On the ninth day, the colossus was balanced on its belly on the top of a pile of stone over eleven feet high. The ten men on the poles were no longer able to reach up to the ends, so they hung on ropes tied to them.

On the tenth day, the statue had reached the required height and they began moving it in the direction of the wall on which it was to stand. This was done at the same indiscernible tempo as before. On the eleventh day they began raising the statue upright, still using stones, but inserting them only under the face, chin and chest. On the eighteenth day, while some pulled on a rope away from the sea, the others held the end of another rope passed round a pole in the middle of the camp, the others began gently levering the statue up. As it rose up in all its imposing height, the pile of stones, relieved of the weight that had held them firm, collapsed and rolled away in a cloud of dust like an avalanche. The statue rocked once and settled, upright.

The huge statue quite altered the look of the place. It was visible from far out to sea. And so, for the first time for a century, a statue stood on the top of *ahu*.

Heyerdahl was still not satisfied: he now wanted to find out how the statues had been transported from the quarry to the coast. Choosing his moment, he asked Pedro Atan who, to his surprise, gave the answer all previous questions had received: "They went there themselves." After much insistence, Pedro eventually explained that his ancestors had used *miro manga erua* to transport the statues. These were sledges, shaped like the letter Y with cross-pieces made of trimmed tree-trunk. They were pulled by ropes made from the bark of the *hau-hau* tree. He then volunteered the suggestion that they try making such a rope and build a sledge. Heyerdahl, of course, was delighted and suggested that they put it to the test by trying to transport one of the recumbent statues. The few descendants of the long-eared ones did not have the strength to pull a loaded sledge and as it was impracticable to engage the entire village, Heyerdahl bought two bullocks which they roasted in the old way over stones in a trough in the ground together with sweet potatoes, maize and pumpkins. Pretty well the entire population was invited to the feast and meanwhile Pedro and his companions got everything ready.

After they had all eaten, 180 of the feasters laid hold of the rope which was fastened to the statue's neck and hauled on it. The rope parted and they all went flat on their backs. They then doubled the rope and this time it held. The statue quivered, then slowly slithered across the grass on its sledge, gaining speed as it went, while Lazarus, Pedro's second-in-command, leaped onto the statue's head from where he gave his orders.

All that remained to discover was how the round stone 'wigs' were placed on the statues' heads. The answer was easy: the tower of stones used to erect the statue acted as scaffolding for the final operation, which was completed using exactly the same primitive methods.

The people who had come to Easter Island all those years ago must have been highly intelligent and practical. They built their statues in accordance with their own traditions and for this they enjoyed peace and endless time. They lived there for hundreds of years having no enemies and no neighbours but fish and whales.

Joining the isthmus of Poike to the rest of the island was the so-called rampart of Iko, a legendary chief. Previous expeditions had refrained from excavating it mainly because previously everyone had agreed that it was a natural geological formation. Even Mrs Scoresby-Routledge after much hesitation had come to this conclusion, though it may at some time have served the long-eared ones for defence. Metraux agreed that it was a natural formation, as did a geologist who saw it. He said that it was formed long before the island was inhabited.

All this did not incline the new expedition to embark on a dig there, but then Father Sebastian admitted to Heyerdahl that be believed the islanders were right in saying that it had been built by their ancestors. The legends about it were too vivid and convincing to have been invented, he said. This decided them to excavate Iko's rampart and the work was supervised by Carlyle Smith. They began by digging five deep square holes. The vertical sections showed conclusively that at some time there had been a giant bonfire there. They then began proper excavation which revealed an artificial trench twelve feet deep and forty feet across at the bottom, which ran along the sides of the volcano for a distance of two kilometres. A giant undertaking. In the ash they found stone missiles and other weapons. The sand and gravel dug out had been used to build up the rampart on the outer edge of the trench, and the way the soil was packed showed that it had been brought up from the trough in woven baskets. Carbon analysis of the charred wood from the fire showed that the war between the short-eared and the long-eared was waged about 1670.

The actual rampart had been built long before the final catastrophe. When the great fires were lit, the trench was already half filled in. At lower levels they found traces of fireplaces and others covered over with earth from the bottom. These builder's fires which were on the hillside dated back to the fourth or fifth century AD, the oldest date ever established for Polynesia.

Heyerdahl spent a great deal of time and energy on trying to solve the puzzle of the island's subterranean caves. Every family had one or more, which served the function of family treasure-chests and sanctuaries. In them they kept the small carvings that were handed down from generation to generation, sometimes in considerable numbers. They were sacred and a taboo protected them from the gaze of the uninitiated. The secret of where they were was likewise passed from father to son, though only to one person in each generation. The superstitious islanders, afraid of the vengeance of Aku-aku, did not want even to discuss these caves and their secret; but Heyerdahl managed to extract various bits of information from them. Eventually he persuaded Pedro Atan and some of his relatives to bring and even sell him a number of old carvings and these proved to be of great ethnological value being unlike anything previously known. Unlike the great statues, these small carvings from the caves showed a great variety of subject: animals, boats, ships, whales, turtles, fish etc. They make it possible to reconstruct a lot of detail about the island's past. For example, on the basis of one unusual, but exact stone model Heyerdahl concluded that the original islanders used reeds to build not only boats, but also large ships that had sails of woven reeds.

The entrances to the caves were not only disguised, but in some cases difficult to negotiate. To enter some you only had to stoop; but others had been deliberately filled in leaving a

square hole just large enough to crawl through on all fours.
Others were even more difficult, you had to go in feet first with
your arms up above your head and so wriggle your way
through. The entrance was always exactly walled in, often
with dressed stones. In some the entrance was like a
horizontal or downward-tilted shaft; with others it was a
chimney leading straight down and you had to brake with
your arms and legs while negotiating it.

Heyerdahl learned to have a torch when entering the
caverns and was able to examine narrow places through which
he had to squeeze. They were all made of smooth blocks of
stone without cement and were rectangular like a chimney.
Some of the chimneys had symmetrical openings and these
proved to have come from the foundations of old huts. In other
words, the people who built them had done so at the cost of
destroying their houses of reed. The entire population of the
island could have found shelter in the caves. Everything
pointed to them having come into use during the civil wars,
when no one dared sleep in his hut and the various entrances
to the caves were held by different families or groups of
families.

It was a long time before even those who were selling
carvings from the caves to Heyerdahl would hear of letting
him see inside these treasure-rooms. When he insisted, they
took him just to the refuge caves of the civil war and it took
months of badgering and many presents before his request
was granted.

On mats placed close together on both sides of the cave lay
the strangest carvings. The cave was only a few yards long,
ending in sheer back walls, but this cave of the Atans was a
real treasure-house. Here were things unknown, things no
museum in the world possessed. The only Polynesian motif
was the man-bird with curved beak and arms behind him.
This, however, he had always seen carved in wood, never in
stone as he did here. There were small stone models of the
paddles typical of Easter Island. Fantastic figures were also
represented: groups carved from one lump, for example two
man-birds holding between them a sort of fairy-tale animal
like a cat. Some figures had heads that did not belong to them
and there were others the sense of which they did not
understand.

Some days before this Lazarus had come to Heyerdahl's
tent with some stones from his cave. He appeared nervous
and already sorry he had come. From a bag he produced

a large bird, the exact image of a penguin. It was life-size and such a perfect likeness the Norwegians were dumbfounded, for Heyerdahl knew that apart from the Antarctic, penguins are only found at the Galapagos. Then Lazarus plunged his hand into his sack again and produced a bird of fantasy, its beak filled with sharp teeth, and, finally, the head of some animal with a badly damaged nose.

The dream of every scientist who goes to Easter Island has been to find another wooden tablet. Today a *kohau rongo-rongo* would be nearly priceless. It would fetch at least 100,000 dollars. The islanders are well aware of this fact and if there was such a thing still hidden in the island it would have been produced by now.

The last one to be obtained was bought by an Englishman. After persuading the islanders to take him to the cave, the Englishman was made to stand behind a line and not cross beyond it, while the islanders went into the cave. This he did. The islanders returned with the tablet and the Englishman bought it, Shortly afterwards the islander went mad and died. All the other islanders are now convinced that this was his punishment for breaking the taboo on the cave of his *rongo-rongo*.

One day an islander called Pakemio, who was the son of the prophetess Angata who had led the revolt that the islanders made when the Scoresby-Routledge expedition was on the island, came to Heyerdahl and told him that when he was a small boy — Pakemio was now an old man! — while with his father on Motu Nui, the bird island, they had hidden a wooden tablet in one of the caves there. Although sceptical, Heyerdahl could not afford not to follow this up and went with the old man to the island. Nothing was found. Some time later, however, Estevar, who was Pedro's uncle, asked Heyerdahl to his hut and there gave him an old, yellowed Chilean school exercise book. It was partially destroyed having, as Estevan explained, been kept for a long time in an old cement bag in the family cave. To Heyerdahl's amazement he found the pages of the exercise book covered with *rongo-rongo* hieroglyphs. Some pages contained only hieroglyphs, others were arranged like a dictionary with explanations in the Easter Island dialect written in clumsy Latin characters opposite each hieroglyph. The exercise book bore the date 1936 and Estevan said that he had been given it by his father just before he died. His father did not know *rongo-rongo* writing and had merely made an exact copy of a still older exercise

hehaga kite kurega.		korara ia koa	
kuaki a rurua.		tagata, mau ahi	
kaka rava		ite miku, nuku ahi	
kuahuki teguru		maitae	
kaki raua,		kua vero, koiaite matā.	
noi a rurua.		maitae. oko mai	
kovaze		kaviri. etakae.	
hemoru. teika		kiuu	
hehaga. kite mea ke		oho	
hehaka. topa hia mai		kerima iruga ite Puoko	
kua oo tetere. ote vaka.		koira koiara kua hai kitoona, ma	
erua oo na. maea kite Puoko.		keoko kekori.	
hekori koi.		kito iko.	

ure vae iku   To ma nha Ava

Part of the headman's book brought back from Easter Island by the Heyerdahl Expedition book inherited from Estevan's grandfather, who had been taught the hieroglyphs and how to cut them on tablets. This he had learned from people, then alive, who had been taught it by priests during the time of the islanders' servitude. The priests had taught it then to the youngest able to learn in an attempt to prevent knowledge of it dying out.

Estevan explained that he had often thought of copying the book before it was altogether ruined, but there were 41 pages and this was more than he could tackle. Heyerdahl then suggested that he copy it by photographing it and after some hesitation, Estevan agreed. Thanks to this, this priceless document has been saved.

Shortly after the expedition left the island, Estevan was lost at sea and it is not known for sure whether the original is still in the family cave, though it was always kept there.

On a second occasion Heyerdahl was presented with a small packet wrapped in reed matting tied with bast. This contained a second faded exercise book, its pages covered with hieroglyphs drawn in ink. Some of the hieroglyphs had explanations in Polynesian written beside them. The last sentence in the book was: "*Kokava aro, kokava tua, te igoa a te akuaku, erua,*" meaning "when destroyed in front and destroyed at the back, make a new one."

Such was the way in which the islanders had tried to preserve their ancient form of writing.

Half-way through 1956, Heyerdahl's expedition left Easter Island for Pitcairn, Mangareva, and the Marquesas in continuation of their search for evidence to support the theory of an American origin for the original inhabitants of the islands of Polynesia.

The scientific value of Heyerdahl's discovery can only be assessed by the experts. The attitude of the academic world has, on the whole, been negative and critical of his unscientific methods.

XVIII

THE THREE THEORIES

There are three theories of the origins of the peoples of the Polynesian islands.

The first theory, accepting the 'autochtonism' of the Polynesians, has it that the islanders are the descendants of the survivors of the people of a legendary drowned continent. The father of this theory, put forward in 1837, was the expert on Tahitian legends, J.A. Moerenhout. He suggested, too, that the Malayan peoples of south-east Asia were of Polynesian origin and not the other way round, as others before him had suggested. He advanced the range of the influence of Polynesian seamen to the coasts of Madagascar. Moerenhout's theory was that the Polynesian islanders thrust the aboriginals of the Indonesian islands, the negritic tribes, into the mountainous interiors.

In support of this idea he asked why, if the Polynesians were of Malayan descent, were the only quadrupeds mentioned in the epics of the Maoris, pigs? The Maoris revere birds, lizards, sharks, but never the crocodile, elephant or tiger or other typical animals of Indonesia and Malaya. Nor do they have any knowledge of alligators, pumas, jaguars or other typical American animals. This implies that they were the aboriginal inhabitants of the islands of Oceania. The track of their migrations were those of the ocean currents of that part of the Pacific, that is from east to west. Despite the vast distances between the archipelagoes of Polynesia, the similarity of the Polynesian dialects is greater than that of heterogenous peoples of the Indonesian islands. Similarly the traditions of the Polynesians about the migrations of their ancestors are astounding in the exact similarity of detail, although recounted by the inhabitants of islands thousands of miles apart. It is interesting that the older the legends or traditions, the more they agree with each other. Almost all Polynesian legends include the story of the great land of Hawaiki that the waves had swallowed up. Hawaiki was said to be the cradle of the Maori people, this being the fatherland from which they were supposed to have sailed to different archipelagoes — *in different directions.*

"They went east to Touamotu and to Maareva (Mangareva) . . . They went to the south to Tupuai (Tubuai), to Femus-ura (islands in the Cook archipelago) and to the farthest fringes of the Maori world (New Zealand) . . . They went to Manitia, Atiu, Aitutati (other islands in the Cook archipelago), to Vavau (Tonga) and farther to Hamoa (Samoa) . . . They went north to distant Nuuhiva (Marquesas) and to flaming Aihi (Hawaii) . . ." to quote the old Tahitian legends recorded by Orsmond.

Attractive as these arguments are, Moerenhout's theory was proved untenable when geological survey of the seabed in the middle of the Pacific showed that as long as Man has existed there has never been a continent there. It is possible that long, long ago one of the larger islands was swallowed up by the sea, which is perfectly possible in that volcanic shelf. Such a cataclysm could well eventually assume continental dimensions in legend.

The second theory is that the Polynesians came to the islands of Oceania from the American continent. One of the most ardent advocates of this theory is Heyerdahl whose ideas were explained at length in the previous chapter.

The third theory is that the Polynesians came from south-east Asia. One supporter of this idea is Te Rangi Hiroa, a Maori doctor who had studied the folklore of his people. After World War Two he began systematically to collect ethnographical data about the Polynesians. On the basis of his own discoveries he came to the conclusion that the ancestors of the present Polynesian islanders arrived in their islands from Indonesia, having been pushed out from there by Mongoloid tribes. It was this fact that first made them take to boats. Later, as they gradually progressed eastward they perfected their seamanship. They first settled the archipelago of Tahiti. All the legends this Maori doctor collected state that the Polynesians came from Hawaiki "the great, the long, the distant" and Te Rangi Hiroa sites the legendary land of Hawaiki in the Society Islands.

Some of the Easter Island legends say that their ancestors came from the east "sailing all the time in the direction of the setting sun" from an archipelago called Marae-toe-hau, meaning "the place of burial". There, it said, the heat was so great that many people died of it and plants and fruits withered. Other indications point to the home of their ancestors having been the island of Oparo, some 4000 kilometres west of Easter Island. Other legends suggest that it could have been Mangareva, one of the Gambier group. It is not impossible that this island was the legendary Maraerenga Hotumatua, but there is no proof.

The most telling arguments against Heyerdahl's hypothesis are those based on the results of athropological research and the analysis of the bone remains of former inhabitants of the island obtained from old graves. An important part in this was played by Professor Godlewski, a Pole, who made a typological analysis of 49 skulls obtained from old megalithic graves on Easter Island. Research over the whole old Polynesian area revealed scarcely 16 per cent of yellow elements, some 34 per cent black and up to 50 per cent of Europeidal, with characteristics related to those of the white race.

This question of the anthropological Europeidal elements in the inhabitants of Easter Island is unusual and mysterious. Nowhere else in all Polynesia is the percentage of Europeidal element (mainly Mediterranean) so high, giving when added to the Oriental element as much as 66.33 per cent. The black, negroidal element (10.21 per cent), the AustroAfrican (8.16 per cent) and Australoid (2.04 per cent) amount together to only 20.41 per cent, while the yellow element is 13.26 per cent. These calculations are based on research on skulls brought back by the German expedition to Easter Island of 1882, by Crawford in 1903 and Scoresby-Routledge in 1914/15. The Mediterranean character of the skulls is so old that it can be compared only to neolithic or even mesolithic skulls found in the Pirenaean peninsula.

It is characteristic that no nordic element was established, despite all the legends telling of a great sailor Tafai, discoverer of a number of new islands, who came from Samoa and was supposed to have had red hair and a ruddy complexion, both characteristics of the fair-haired nordic peoples who tan puce. It is obvious from the accounts of many visitors to Easter Island that the proportion of red-haired people must always have been considerable. Another Easter Island characteristic is the people's height (average 173.3 centimetres) the greatest of any of the peoples of Oceania with the exception of the inhabitants of Rarotonga where it is 174.4 centimetres.

Analysis using the methods of Polish anthropologists (Czekanowski, Michalski and Wanke) led Godlewski to the conclusion that Polynesian seamen's migrations were made in three phases: in the first they went from Asia through Micronesia towards the Solomon Islands and the New Hebrides to the islands of Tonga and Samoa and to New Zealand — all this before the Christian era. This is confirmed by the results of archaeological research which has shown that the stone tools of this age of Indonesia and Polynesia are identical.

The second wave of migration had two starting points: the islands of Tonga and Samoa. The seamen of this wave reached the Cook Islands and the Marquesas. Because there are no sanscrit elements in Polynesian dialects, Professor Godlewski considers that the ancestors of the Polynesians left the islands of Indonesia before the Christian era, because the Hindu influence in Indonesia goes back to the first century.

Godlewski makes Tahiti and Hawaii the centres of the third phase of Polynesian migration. This last phase, directed towards central Polynesia from the south, brought with it many elements of yellow races, which eventually became stratified and mixed with old Polynesian elements.

Interestingly, the results of anthropological research agree entirely with those of linguistic research. An American scholar, William Churchill, one of the most eminent in the field of comparative linguistics, reached similar conclusions. It is, perhaps, worth noting here that Gonzales' Spanish expedition of 1770 recorded a few words of the Easter Islanders' tongue, especially the numbers and these are quite different to those used today. Neither do they have any particular Polynesian sound, which would seem to point to them being the remains of some archaic tongue spoken by the earliest inhabitants of the island.

Wagner (1937) said that the Easter Islanders were a mixture of Melanesian and Polynesian. Meyer and Jablonowski, however, see only one wave reaching Easter Island. Thus scholars are far from agreeing and the mysteries of the island remain largely unsolved.

Many European scholars see a considerable similarity between the culture of Easter Island, art, writing and artefacts, with those of south-east Polynesia, New Zealand and the Marquesas, especially between the island's stone statues and the Solomon Island carvings.

The bas-reliefs found especially at Orongo depict human figures with birds' heads, yet these heads are not those of the tern, which was revered on the island and in whose honour the carvings were made. The scholarly opinion is that these long-legged birds with thick backs and protruberant crops point to a Melanesian origin of this bird cult. A similar cult developed in the Solomon Islands and spread throughout Melanesia. Its object was the frigate bird which has perhaps the greatest flight endurance of any sea bird. The Easter Island bas-reliefs clearly have both the beak and the craw of the frigate bird, the range of which does not extend to treeless Easter Island. The frigate bird nests only in trees. One of the *rongo-rongo* hieroglyphs is the frigate bird symbol.

Metraux thought that their racial characteristics showed the Easter Islanders to be typically Polynesian and that there was no need to seek for similarities with the peoples of Melanesia. But the Russian scholar, Professor Tokariev, whose speciality is Polynesian affairs, considers that though there is sufficient evidence to support Metraux' conclusion, that is no reason to give up looking for historical links with other, more distant areas both in Asia and America. He feels that one cannot say that the argument has been concluded, at any rate not until analysis of the *rongo-rongo* hieroglyphs and those of Mohenzo-Dara are complete, for here science has not yet said the last word.

In 1948 Werner Wolff published his paper on the *rongo-rongo* hieroglyphs. He had compared them with Egyptian hieroglyphs both for shape and meaning. This showed that 86 hieroglyphs from the tablets bore a striking resemblance in pictorial content and meaning to the ideogramic hieroglyphs of ancient Egypt.

Professor Thomas S. Barthel of the University of Hamburg, a specialist in Polynesian problems, became so intrigued by the mysterious Easter Island writing that he determined to try and decipher it. Having discovered that there was no publication in which all twety-five surviving tablets were reproduced he wrote to all the museums concerned asking for legible pictures, photographs or plaster-casts of them and before long he had a complete collection which gave him more than 12,000 hieroglyphs.

First, Barthel catalogued and numbered the individual signs. By the time he had finished he was so familiar with them that he could start arranging them in groups and sub-groups, reducing their numbers by eliminating those that were repeated. By dividing the signs into letters, syllables, words and sentences, he came to the conclusion that *rongo-rongo* writing consisted of 20-30 basic signs comparable to an alphabet. By various combinations it was possible to built about 100 syllables.

The next step was to try and attach meanings to the hieroglyphs and for this Barthel felt that he must have recourse to Bishop Jaussen's reports which would seem to have the most accurate of any. It then transpired that the authorities of the Church had so successfully hidden the pagan songs of Metoro that no one could tell him where they were or whether they still existed.

Undeterred, the Professor embarked on a search worthy of any detective which led from Tahiti through France and Belgium to the Vatican. Finally he found the bishop's notebooks in a monastery in the little town of Grottaferrata not far from Rome. As Barthel wrote, they proved to be his Rosetta stone.

First, Barthel made a carfeul comparison of Jaussen's notes with the texts of the four tablets Metoro had read to the bishop. He was greatly helped here by his knowledge of polynesian dialects. Gradually he achieved a text that began to make sense. His first discovery here was that the symbols for sun and moon were always preceded by abstract signs of two sticks, which reminded him that in Maori and Polynesian mythology the sun and moon are always represented as twins and these heavenly twins are often referred to metaphorically as the "two sticks".

The more he came to know about the four tablets, the more he understood why Metoro's songs seemed unintelligible babbling to the poor bishop. Metoro of course was in the position of a schoolboy who is asked to explain a university text book. Having only a superficial knowledge of the hieroglyphs, he had read some correctly, but had had to guess at the meaning of others and as a result had produced a text that was devoid of sense.

Barthel came to the conclusion that the *rongo-rongo* is a proper form of writing. Its signs are subject to definite formal rules, which is not the case with the pictorial writing of some Indian tribes of America. Most ancient systems of writing have sought to reduce their symbols to purely abstract lines, but Easter Island writing consists largely of stylized outlines of diagrammatic objects. Its basic elements include certain shapes of heads, body-positions corresponding to pantomime expressions, while unusual characteristic stylization of the hands and arms would seem to suggest a language of gesture. Animals and plants are represented more or less naturalistically. Yet many of the geometrical signs are so contracted that it is not possible accurately to determine their meaning.

Easter Island writing consists of 120 basic elements which are combined in a variety of ways to give more than 1000 compound signs.

Most of the signs are used as ideograms, usually in the form of words. Thus the element divided means the word 'art', a sleeping bird means the word 'death', a line in characteristic white colour acts for the word 'white'. The language is frequently metaphorical and poetic: a flower means 'woman' and 'firstborn son' is depicted by a beautiful ornament.

The writers of Easter Island took a first step towards a phonetic writing, expressing abstract concepts in the way of the rebus today. Polynesian languages being on the whole rich in homonyms, their writers could often use concrete words meaning an abstraction. For example they used the picture of an oyster to mean prayer, because the word for oyster, *pure*, was phonetically the same as that for prayer. Similarly, the pictogram 'dancing paddle', *rapa*, also meant 'splendour' and the symbol for material of woven bark, *tapa*, also meant 'to count'.

Here are some words from Professor Barthel's dictionary:

	Sign	Pronounciation	Meaning
Simple signs		*Toki*	Small axe
		Vai	Water
		Tangata	Person
Compound signs		*Rutu te Pahu*	Strike a drum
		Kohau rongo-rongo	Talking tablet
Adjectival signs		*Koti*	Average
		Moe	Sleeping, dead
		Tea	White
Metaphorical expressions		*Pua*	(1) Flower (2) Woman
		Rei kura	(1) Precious ornament (2) First-born son

	Sign	Pronunciation	Meaning
Examples of	()	*Pure*	(1) Oyster
rebus			(2) Prayer
writing	8	*Rape*	(1) Dancing paddle
			(2) Excellence
	(	*Tapa*	(1) Bark, woven material
			(2) To count

Professor Barthel considered that the Easter Island writing did not have time to mature and develop into a phonetic system capable of expressing the whole sentence to be spoken. As a result, the tablets reduced the songs to contracted form, like a telegram or a charade, which merely indicated the sense of the text leaving it to the reciter to fill in the missing words. No wonder, then, that they are extraordinarily difficult to read today.

Here is part of the text of one tablet translated by Professor Barthel:

Signs

Polynesian text   *Pu, rutu te pahu, rei, kura, atariki, henva, toko rangi, tane*

Translation   Blow the shell trumpet and beat the drum
For the precious ornament
For the first born of this world
For the support of the heavens
For Tane

In 1958 Professor Barthel published an article summarizing the results of his work in *Scientific American*. To everyone's surprise, he announced that the surviving tablets had been mostly religious or cult texts and that there was scarcely any mention of historical events affecting Easter Island. Barthel had discovered that the islanders had another kind of writing, called *tau*, solely devoted to recording the chronicles and other lay matters. Unfortunately, no examples of this had survived. The surviving tablets contained mostly hymns in honour of the gods, instruction to priests, etc. These cult accounts show that the idyllic-sounding island had been the scene not only of internecine strife, but also of cannabalism, the victims including children. None of the texts Barthel translated threw any new light on other Easter Island mysteries, certainly not on the people's origin or the significance of the giant statues.

The character of the writing shows, in Barthel's opinion, that it was not invented on Easter Island, but brought there. He was brought to this conclusion by the fact that many of the signs depict plants and animals which have never existed in Easter Island. The signs also point undoubtedly to a Polynesian (and not an American) origin. For example: in the texts the symbol of the breadfruit tree figures repeatedly and this tree was never grown on Easter Island, but was long the basic food of the inhabitants of many of the Polynesian islands. Many stylistic details are strikingly similar to the wooden carvings of the old Maori artists of New Zealand and the Marquesas.

Sure proof of Polynesian origin has been provided by Barthel's deciphering of a number of geographical names in the tablets, eg. Rangi-tea (now the island of Raiatea in the Society Islands), and of gods and temples on the islands of Tahiti and Borabora. Even the ancient name of Pitcairn Island is mentioned, this probably being the last stage in the Polynesian migration eastwards before reaching Easter Island.

But Barthel has not found an answer to the questions: who invented this form of writing and why it has survived only on Easter Island?

CONCLUSION

Easter Island, the most isolated place in the world, is moving with giant strides into the atomic age. It has been selected to be made into an important link for air-sea communications between South America and New Zealand and Australia. For some years work has been going on building a giant trans-ocean airport, a fact that has considerably disquieted the world of learning, for what will happen to the carvings and stone terraces when miles of concrete runways have to be built? Easter Island is really a giant open-air museum and, surely, ought to be made an international reserve or park of relics, as has been done with the Galapagos Islands.

Perhaps more disquieting is the interest being taken in the island by American military authorities. The larger units of the US fleet, especially the giant aircraft carriers, are unable because of their size to use the Panama Canal and so have to go round the tip of South America to get from the Pacific to the Atlantic or vice versa. There is no base along the 7000 miles between Cape Horn and Pearl Harbour, hence the attention of American strategists has been turned to lonely Easter Island, which lies roughly at two-thirds of the way. Latin America and especially Chile do not like the idea of any such development. Nothing has yet been decided, and, meanwhile Chile tries to administer the island as well as its modest means allow. More islanders are going to the mainland to study and returning as qualified teachers and doctors, but only a radical change in the island's economic state could improve the lot of the islanders as they deserve.

The Chilean authorities would like to turn Easter Island into another Hawaii, making it a world tourist centre, and towards this in 1967 they started a service of regular sailings between the island and the mainland until such time as the airport is built. They would like to see Easter Island an open-air museum and in the plan an important element is the restoration and re-erection of the stone statues, a very laborious and costly business. In an attempt to help Chile here, UNESCO called in Professor William Mulloy of Wyoming, an anthropologist, and Charles Peterson, an architect, and they have listed the statues able to be restored — more than 1000 of them, some weighing 80 tons and about 350 *ahu* platforms. Also included in the plan are a dozen old villages with stone foundations that show them to have been the sites of earlier settlements.

Having compiled their list, the next thing was to see if the work was practicable and in 1960 Mulloy and a Chilean archaeologist, Gonzalo Figueroa, began restoring an *ahu*, that at Akivi. The primitive tools used by the old Easter Islanders were used: eg. stones and levers of long baulks of eucalyptus. It took them a whole month to erect the first of seven 15-ton statues; but practice making perfect, the last one took just under a week to put in place. The greatest difficulty, however, is that of topping the statues with their red hair-dos.

The government plan includes the building of a large ethnographic museum at Hanga Roa.

As civilization comes to Easter Island, where Spanish is the language of administration, the islanders are losing more and more of their individuality. The Catholic religion has eradicated the old beliefs and customs. Though they have a certain nationalistic pride, especially over the mystery of their origins, they learn of their traditions really only from books. Now, the only real source of further information is the ground of the island and what the archaeologists find there.

The *rongo-rongo* tablets have been more or less deciphered, but it would appear that *tau* writing has been completely lost and for ever.

CHRONOLOGY OF EVENTS

1566   Supposed discovery of Easter Island by Mendana.

1686   Supposed discovery by Davis in *Bachelor's Delight*.

6th April
1722   Discovery by Dutch expedition under Roggeveen.

1770   Spaniards take possession of the island and name it San Carlos.

1774   Visited by Captain Cook.

1756   La Pérouse lands on the island.

1805   American schooner *Nancy* forcibly carries off 12 men and 10 women.

1806   Islanders prevent landing from Kaaku-Manu.

1811   The second officer of American ship, *Pindos*, shoots an islander.

1816   Islanders prevent Otto Kotzebue and the Russian expedition landing.

1825   Visit by F.W. Beechey in *Blossom*.

1830   French landing.

1862   Lejeune, captain of French ship *Cassini*, makes the first investigation among the islanders.

1862   Massacre and enslavement of islanders by Peruvian slavers.

1864   French missionaries settle on the island.

1868   *Topaze* takes the first statue from Easter Island back to the British Museum.

1869   Plantation started on island.

1870   Visit by Chilean corvette *O'Higgins*.

1871   Visit by N. Miklucho-Maklaj.

1872   *La Flore* takes the head of a statue back to museum in Paris.

1875	*O'Higgins* pays a second visit.
1877	Adolphe Pinard, a Frenchman, conducts investigations.
1877	American ship, *Black Eagle*, wrecked on the island and her crew spend involuntary 6 months there.
1879	Salmon takes over from Dutroux-Bornier and conducts search for antiquities on a large scale.
1882	British warship *Sapho* visits the island.
1882	German gunboat *Hyena* visits the island and Weisser discovers paintings at Orongo and buys objects for German museums.
1886	American ship visits the island. W. Thomson investigates and removes a statue to Washington.
1888	Chile takes possession of the island.
1889	*O'Higgins* pays a third visit.
1895	*O'Higgins* pays a fourth visit.
1897	H. Merlet, a Chilean industrialist, starts sheepshearing on a large scale. Later taken over by Williamson and Balfour.
1901	French *La Durance* visits the island. Dr Delabaude conducts the first archaeological dig and examines skulls etc. from graves. Makes a collection of interesting photographs.
1904	First geological investigation made by Alexander Agassiz.
1905	Meteorological, seismological and ethnographic work done by Chilean team. Statue removed to Chile.
1914-16	Investigations by Scoresby-Routledges.
1914	Chilean ship sent to quell revolt headed by Angata. Henceforward Chilean ships pay annual visits.
1916	German warships spend six weeks at island. Sink French sailing ship *Jean.*
1916-18	Examination by Father Edwards and Bienvenido de Estella
1923	Ethnological studies by McMilan Brown.
1925	Baron von Teuber's mission.
1930	Swedish botanist Skottsberg works in island.
1931	Brief visit by American, Casey, who publishes an account of his visit.
1932	American Museum of Natural History sends Templeton Crocke to island.

1934	Franco-Belgian team works in island.
1955-56	Heyerdahl and his team on island.
1959	Russian expedition to island in *Ob*.
1960	Dr Mulloy and Gonzalo Figueroa reconstruct an *ahu*.
1961	American Geographical Society's expedition.

LIST OF THE LEGENDARY KINGS
OF EASTER ISLAND

1	Hotumatua	30	Kote Kura Tahoua
2	Tuumaeheke	31	Taoraha Kaihahanga
3	Nuku	32	Tukuma
4	Miru	33	Tekahui te Hunga
5	Hiuariru	34	Tetun Hunga Nui
6	Aturangi	35	Tetun Hunga Noa
7	Raa	36	Tetu Hunga Mare Kapeau[2]
8	Atarauga	37	Toati Rangi Hahe[2]
9	Hakapuna	38	Tagaroa Tatarara
10	Oihu	39	Hariui Koro
11	Ruhoi	40	Punahako
12	Tukanga te Mamaru	41	Puna Ate Tuu
13	Takahita	42	Puna Kai te Vaua
14	Ouraraa	43	Teriri Ketea
15	Koroharua	44	Haumoena
16	Mahuta Ariiki[1]	45	Tupeari Ki
17	Atua Ure Rangi	46	Mahiki Tapuekiti
18	Teriri Turkua	47	Tuu Koiho
19	Korua-Rongo	48	Anekena
20	Tiki-Tehatu	49	Nui Tupahotu
21	Urukenu	50	Re Kauu
22	Teruruatiki te Hatu	51	Terava Rara
23	Nau Ta Mahiki	52	Tehitehuke
24	Terika Tea	53	Terahai
25	Terio Kautahito	54	Kaimokoi
26	Kotepu Ite Toki	55	Ngaara
27	Kote Hiti Ruanea	56	Kaimakoi
28	Turua Ki Kena	57	Maurata[3]
29	Tuterkimanara	58	Gregorio (Kerekoio Rokoroko)[4]

1. Mahuta Ariiki had a son called Tuii (or Tro)-ko-iho, who was the first sculptor of stone statues. He died before his father.

2. These two kings ruled simultaneously, the son having revolted against his father whom eventually he killed.

3. King Maurata died in exile on Chincha island, Peru. He had two sons, Tepito and Kerekorio, but they never ruled.

4. Did not rule. He died among the French missionaries.

BIBLIOGRAPHY

General

BACHE Rene, Easter Island. A strange land in the South Sea. Goldthwaite's Geographic Magazine, New York 1892, p. 276-282.
BARCLAY H.V., Easter Island and colossal statues. Proceedings of the Royal Geographical Society of Australasia (South Australasian Branch) 1899, p. 127 and 146.
BARCLAY H.V., Mission à l'Ile de Paques. C. Rd. de la Soc. de Geogr. de Paris 1899, p. 169-176.
CHAUVET Stephen, L'Ile de Pacques et ses Mysteres, Paris 1935 (p. 83-86 gives a full bibliography to 1935.)
COOKE Georges, Te Pito te Henua, Known as Rapa-Nui, commonly called Easter Island. Report of the US National Museum for 1897, p. 689-723. Smithonian Institution Washington, 1899.
GANA G., Descripcion cientifica de la Isla de Pascua. Revista de la Marina. Vol. I. p. 368 and 460. Valparaiso 1885.
LUKE H., Islands of the South Pacific, London 1962.
MACHOWSKI Jacek, Wyspa Tajemnic, "Problemy" No. 8/1955, p. 529-538.
MACHOWSKI Jacek, Wyspa Tajemnic, "Problemy" No. 8/1955, p. 529-538.
MAZIERE Francis, Fantastique ile de Pâques, Paris 1966, Edition Robert Lafont.
REPORTAJE a la Isla de Pascua, fotografias de Rebeca Yanez, textos de Enrique Bello, Revista de Arte, Universidad de Chile, Santiago de Chile Marzo-Junio de 1957.

Particular

Chapter 2

BEHRENS Karl Friedrich, Histoire de l'Expedition de trois vaisseaux, envoyes par la Compagnie des Indes occidentales des Provinces unies aux Terres Australes, en 1721, 2 vols., La Haye, 1739.

At the present moment the bibliography of Easter Island comprises several hundred entries. Here only the more important of the works consulted are listed. Those wishing to consult the full bibliography are referred to Alfred Metraux, *Ethnology of Easter Island*, Bernice P. Bishop Museum, Honolulu, Bulletin 160, 1940.

INFANZONI Aguera, Manuscrit original de la decouverte de l'Isle de Davis, a bord de le fregate Santa-Rosalia, du 10 octobre 1770 au 29 mars 1771.
ROGGEVEEN Jacob, Histoire de l'expedition de trois vaisseaux, La Haye 1739 (*see* below Gonzalez y Haedo).

Chapter 3

GONZALEZ y HAEDO Felipe, The voyage of Captain Don Felipe Gonzalez in the Ship of the Line "San Lorenzo" with the Frigate "Santa Rosalia" in Company to Easter Island, in 1770-1771, preceded by an Extract from Mynheer Jacob Roggeveen's Official Log of his Discovery of an Visit to Easter Island in 1722, transcribed, translated and edited by Bolton Glanvill Corney. Cambridge 1908, Hakluyt Society.

Chapter 4

COOK James, Second Voyage towards the South Pole and round the World, performed in the "Resolution" and "Adventure" 1772-75, London 1777.
FORSTER George, A Voyage round the World in H.B.M.'s Sloop "Resolution" during the year 1772, London 1777.

Chapter 5

LA PEROUSE Jean Francois de Galaup, Voyage de la Perouse autour du monde (1785-1788). Paris, imp. de la Republique, (1797).

Chapter 6

CHAMISSO Adalbert, Bemerkungen und Ansichten auf einer Entdeckungsreise unter Kotzebue, 1828. Beschreibung einer Reise um die Welt.
LISIANSKY J.F., Voyage round the world 1803-1806, London 1814.
KRUSENSTERN I. F., Voyage, autour du monde, fait dans les annees 1803, 1804, 1805, 1806 par ordre de S.M.I. Alexandre 1 er Empereur de Russie, sur les vaissaux la "Nadiejda" et la "Neva", commandes par M. de Krusenstern, Capitaine de Vaissau de la Marine Imperiale. Librairie Gide Fils, Paris 1821.

Chapter 7

BEECHEY Frederick William, Narrative of a Voyage to the Pacific and Behring's Straits, London 1931, 2 vols.

Chapters 8 and 9

see General Bibliography

Chapter 10

EYRAUD Eugene, Rapport sur l'Ile de Pâques, Annales de la Propagation de la Foi, vol. 38, Lyon 1866, pp. 44-71 and 124-145, vol. 39, Lyon 1867, p. 250-259.
MOULY R.P. SS. CC. L'ile de Pâques, Ile de Mystère et d'Heroisme, Paris 1948.
ROUSSEL Hippolyte R.P., Ile de Pâques, our Rapa Nui (1869). Notes published in Annales des Sacrés-Coeurs, February, June 1926, Braine le-Comte (Belgium).

Chapter 11

JAUSSEN Tepano, Ile de Pâques, historique et ecriture par Mgr. Tepano Jaussen, Eveque d'Axieeri, premier vicaire apostolique de Tahiti, Oceanie (MS illustrated by the author and written about 1885 is in the Congregation Sacres-Couers de Picpus in Braine-le-Comte, Belgium).
JAUSSEN Tepano, L'ile de Pâques, Historique et Ecriture, Bulletin de Geographie No 2/1893, Paris.
JAUSSEN Tepano, Quatre "Kohau rongo-rongo" (MS deposited in the Library if the Society for Ocean Research in Paris.) 1894.
MIKLUCHO-MAKLAJ Nikolaj Nikolajewica, Sobranije soczinienij w pjati tomach, Moskwa, Izdatielstwo Akademii Nauk SSSR, 1950-1954.
MIKLUCHO-MAKLAJ Nikolaj Nikolajewicz, O "kohau rongo-rongo ili derewjannych tablicach s ostrowa Rapa-nui (translation of an article published in Zeitschrift der Gesellschaft fur Erdkunde, vol. 7, 1872, p. 79-81) Sobranie soczinienij . . . vol. III/cz. 1, p. 482-484.
MIKLOUHO-MACLAY N.N., Sur les Kohau rongo-rongo de Rapanui. Nouvelles de la Societe de Geographie de Russie, vol. VIII, 1872, No 2, p. 42-55.
MIKLUCHO-MAKLAJ Mikolaj, Podróże, translated from the Russian by Andrzej Milosz, Warszawa 1952, Ksiazka i Wiedza.

Chapter 12

GEISELER, Die Oster-Insel. Eine Statte prähistorischer Kultur in der Sudsee. Bericht des Kommandanten S. M. Kbt. "Hyane", Kapitanlieutenant Geiseler uber die ethnologische Untersuchung der Oster-Insel (Rapanui) an den Chef der Kaiserlichen Admiralität. Berlin 1883.

Chapter 13

THOMSON William J., Te Pito te Henua, or Easter Island, by Paymaster William J. Thomson, U. S. Navy, Annual Report of the Board of Regents of the Smithonian Institution for the year 1888/89. Washington 1891, p. 447-452.

Chapter 14

SCORESBY-ROUTLEDGE Katherine, The Mystery of Easter Island, The story of an expedition, London 1919.
SCORESBY-ROUTLEDGE Katherine, Survey of the Village and Carved Rocks of Orongo, Easter Island, by the Mana Expedition, Journal of the Royal Anthropological Institute, London, vol. 50/1920, p. 425-451.

Chapter 15

LAVACHERY Henri, Ile de Paques, Paris, B. Grasset 1935.
METRAUX Alfred, Easter Island, A. Stone-Age Civilization of the Pacific, New York 1957.

Chapter 16

BUTINOW N.A. i KNOROZOW Y.V., Wstępny raport o studiach nad językiem pisanym Wyspy Wielkanocnęy. (Paper read in May 1956 at the Ethnological Conference in Leningrad.)
EZOW Edward, Na Wyspie Wielkanocnej. "Nowe Czasy", nos 22 and 29, May 1959, p. 27-28.
KUDRIAWCEW Borys G., Pismiennost' ostrowa Paschi. Sbornik Muzeja Antropologii i Etnograffi, wyd. Akademii Nauk ZSRR, vol XI, 1949, p. 176-221.
OLDEROGGE D.A., Parallelnyje teksty tablic ostrowa Paschi. Sbornik Muzeja Antropologii i Etnografii, vol. XI, 1949, p. 222-236.
OLDEROGGE D.A., Parallelnyje teksty niekotorych Jeroglificzeskich tablic s ostrowa Paschi. Sowietskaja Etnografija, Akademii Nauk ZSRR, No 4/1946, p. 234-238.
RACHTANOW I., Potomki Maklaja, Moskwa-Leningrad, 1954.

Chapter 17

ARCHAEOLOGY of Easter Island, Stockholm, Forum A. B. 1961.
(Composite work by five archaeologists and members of the Heyerdahl Expedition.)

HEINE-GELDERN Robert, Heyerdahl's Hypothesis of Polynesian Origins: a Criticism, The Geographical Journal, London, vol. 116, No 4-6/1950, p. 183-192.

HEYERDAHL Thor, American Indians in the Pacific, Stockholm, Forum A. B. 1952.

HEYERDAHL Thor, Wyprawa Kon-Tiki, Warszawa 1960, Iskry.

HEYERDAHL Thor, Aku-Aku. Tajemnica Wyspy Wielkanocnej, Warszawa 1959, Iskry.

REPORTS of the Norwegian Archaeological Expedition to Easter Island and the East Pacific, Thor Heyerdahl and Edwin N. Ferdon jr. Research and the Kon-Tiki Museum (Oslo-Norway) No 24/1965, Santa Fe, New Mexico, USA.

Chapter 18

ANDREJEWA K., Tajemnice zaginionych lądów, Wiedza Powszechna, Warszawa 1956.

BARTHEL Thomas S., The "Talking Boards" of Easter Island, "Scientific American", June 1958, p. 61-68.

CARROLL A., The Easter Island. Inscriptions and the way in which they are translated or deciphered and read. The Journal of the Polynesian Society. London 1892, p. 102.

CHURCHILL William, Easter Island, The Rapanui speech and the peopling, of Southeast Polynesia. The Carnegie Institution of Washington 1912.

ENGLERT P. Sebastian, Tradiciones de la Isla de Pascua en idioma rapanui y castellano. Padre Las Casas. imper. y edit... San Francisco 1939.

ENGLERT P. Sebastian, La tierra de Hotu-Matu'a. Historia, etnologia y lengua de la Isla de Pascua. Padre Las Casas, impr. y edit. San Francisko 1948.

GODLEWSKI Aleksander Lech, Charakterystyka antropologiczna dawnych mieskanców Wyspy Wielkanocnej, "Przegląd Antropologiczny", Warszawa-Poznan, vol. XX/1954, p. 105-126.

GODLEWSKI Aleksander Lech, Struktura antropologiczna Polinezyjczyków, PWN, Wróclaw 1955.

HARLEZ C., L'lle de Paques et ses Monuments graphiques. Istas, Lonvain 1895.

HEVESY W., Osterinselschrift und Indusschrift, Oriental Lit. Ztg. November 1934 (English translation, The Easter Island and the Indus valley script, "Anthropos" 33, 1938, part 5-6).

LAFAY Howard, Easter Island and Its Mysterious Monuments, National Geographic, vol. 121, No 1, January 1962, p. 90-117.

UZIN S., Zagadkowe lady, Wiedza Powszechna, Warszawa 1952.

VOLTZ Wilhelm, Analyse de 49 cranes pascuans, Archiv fur Anthropologie, vol. XXIII, November 1894, p. 97-169.

WOLFF W., Island of Death. A new Key to Easter Island's Culture. J. J. Augustin Publication. New York 1948.

INDEX

Adams, Alexander, 63-4
Adventure, 41
Afrikaansche Galei, 17-22
agriculture, 36, 53, 55, 66, 97
ahu, see platforms, stone
Akahanga, 86
Aku-aku, 188
Alaska, 57, 65
Alexander I, Tsar, 57
Amat, Don Manuel de, 29, 30
American expedition, 125-43
Anakena, 73, 80, 81, 84, 85, 91, 92, 93, 130, 141, 176, 177
Anapika Bay, 100
ancestors, 83; *see also* origins of the Polynesian islanders
Anga Piko, 74
Angata, 150-2, 190
Antarctic Ocean, 41
archaeological work, 176, 178-81, 187-8
Areauti, 96-7
Arend, 17-19, 21
Argentine, 89, 147
Ariki Oroi, 83-6
arikis, 45
Arriaga, Don Julian de, 29, 30
Astrolabe, 49, 54
astronomical observatory, 180-1
Atan, Juan, 173
Atan, Pedro, 160, 182-7, 188
Atua, 183
Atua Vre Rangei, 74
Avareipua, 85

Bachelor's Delight, 17
Barnabe, Captain P., 102

Barthel, Professor Thomas S., 197-201
bas-reliefs, 127, 130, 196-7
Bastian, Professor, 117
Batavia, 27
Beechey, Captain Frederick William, 65, 66, 67, 70
Benson, Captain, 147
Bering Straits, 65
Blossom, 65
boats, islanders', 26, 61, 99, 129, 188
Borabora, 201
Bornier, *see* Dutroux-Bornier
Bougainville (explorer), 30, 49
Bouman, Captain, 19, 20
Boussole, 49
Bouvet (explorer), 49
Braine-le-Comte, museum at, 170
Brander, Mr, 105-6, 109, 110, 112, 118, 125, 128, 130, 140
Brazil, 147
Brest, 50
British Museum, 147, 170
bustrefedon, 113, 114, 115, 157n
Butinov, Professor, 172
Byron (explorer), 30

Callao de Lima, 30, 31
Camp Mohican, 128
Canada, 65
Canary Islands, 147
Cape Ahuakapu, 129
Cape Anakoirangaroa, 128
Cape Horn, 65

218   *Island of Secrets*

Cape Pokokoria, 131
Cape Verde, 147
Captain Benson's Own Story, 147
capture of islanders, 63-4, 67
Carter (explorer), 30
carvings, wooden, 46, 188
caverns, subterranean, 37, 46, 53, 119; explored by Thor Heyerdahl, 188-9
Celebes, 115
Chamisso, Adelbert von, 62-3
Champsaur, 89
Charles III, 30
Chile, 18, 50, 63, 65, 89, 90, 102, 107, 117, 148, 150, 152, 157, 163-4, 203
Chincha Island, 82, 88, 90, 209
Chinese symbols, 158
Churchill, William, 196
Clair, Father, 90, 91
clothing, islanders', 21, 23-4, 31, 45, 62
Clouard (ship's second-in-command), 54
Congregation of the Sacred Heart, 89, 90, 102, 109
Cook, Captain James, 41-7, 53
Cook Bay, 58, 59, 63, 93, 125, 145, 148, 152
Cook Islands, 194, 196
Cooper, First Officer, 41
copeca, 33
Copenhagen, 109
Copiapo, 90
Cornwall, dolmens of, 158
Crozet (explorer), 49
curiologics, 113, 114, 115
Curti, Arnoldo, 177
Cusco, palace at, 158
Czernuskow, Valery, 169

Dampier, William, 17, 21
Daniel, 91, 92
dating, carbon, 180, 188
David's Island, 30, 31
Davis, Edward, 17-18, 21
'Descendants of Maklaj', 169-73
Diringer, David, 171

Domonte, Don Antonio, 30, 31
Dorion, Fernando, 172
Drapkin, Dr, 167
Dutch East Indies, 26-7
Dutch expedition, 17-27
Dutroux-Bornier, 105-6, 110, 118, 145

ear-ornaments, 21, 24
East India Company, 17, 27
Easter Island: Dutch discovery of, 17-27; naming of, 19, 38; Spanish expedition to, 29-39, 50; first map of, 35, 36, 50; English expeditions to, 41-7, 65-71, 145-56; French expeditions to, 49-56; Russian expeditions to, 57-64, 172-3; setting up of missions on, 89-106; Easter Island Company, 107, 149-52; German visit to, 117-24; American expedition to, 125-43; Franco-Belgian expedition to, 157-67; Thor Heyerdahl's expedition to, 175-92; future of, 203-4
Easter islanders: agriculture of, 36, 53, 55, 66, 97; appearance of, 24, 34, 61, 62, 68, 160; boats of, 26, 61, 99, 129; capture of, 63-4, 67, 177; clothing of, 21, 23-4, 31, 45, 62; ear-ornaments of, 21, 24; homes of, 25-6, 36, 37, 46, 53, 54, 66, 94; language of, 42, 114, 196; linguistic skills of, 35, 38; preparation of food by, 25, 126-7; religious beliefs of, 24, 45, 53, 135; thieving propensities of, 22, 34, 43, 51-2, 54, 55-6, 62, 68, 69, 95-7, 100-1, 161, 162, 164, 173

Edmunds, Percy, 145-7, 148, 150, 151
El Dorado, 146, 147
Englert, Father Sebastian, 173, 178, 182, 187
English expeditions, 41-7, 65-71, 146-56
Escolan, Theodale, 105
Escuere, Lieutenant d', 52
Estevan, 190, 192
Ethnological Museum, Santiago, 110
Eyraud, Brother Eugene, 13, 89-105, 111
Eyraud, Jean, 90

Farrera, Carlos Rivera, 172
Favorite, 90
Ferdon, Edwin, 178, 180, 181
Figueroa, Gonzalo, 204
food, preparation of, 25, 126-7
Forster (naturalist), 42, 46
Franco-Belgian expedition, 157-67
Franklin, Captain John, 65
French expeditions, 49-56
funeral, 81

Galapagos Island, 176, 190
Galaup, Captain Jean François de, *see* La Pérouse, Count of
Gambier, Captain, 103
Gambier archipelago, 91, 102, 106
Gana, Captain, 110, 140
Geiseler, Captain, 117, 118, 119, 123
General Baquedano, 151
German visits, 117-24, 152-3
Gillam, Captain, H.J., 145
Godlewski, Professor, 195-6
Gonzalez y Haedo, Don Felipe, 30-1, 33, 34
Great Museum of Anthropology and Ethnography, 169
Grottaferrata, 198
guano-digging, 81-2, 90, 177

Haapape, plantation at, 106, 112
Haka-rongo-manu, 80
Hana, 77
Hango Piko, 100, 101, 102, 118, 120
Hango Roa, 81, 91, 92, 95, 101, 102, 103, 105, 106, 110, 119, 123, 128, 148, 159, 163, 164, 165, 167, 172; museum at, 204
Hanga-te-tenga, 86
Hangaone Bay, 131
Hau-maka, 84
Hawaii, 194, 196
Hawaiki, 193-4
Heine-Geldern (sinologist), 158
Hevesy, William, 157
Heyerdahl, Thor, 173, 175-92, 195
hieroglyphs, 13-15, 97, 111-15, 140, 141, 142-3, 153-5, 157-8, 190-2, 197-201; deciphering of, 14, 112-15, 169-73, 197-201
Hirapote, 112
homes, islanders', 25-6, 36, 37, 46, 53, 54, 66, 94
hopu, 76-80
Hotumatua, legend of king, 83-8, 112, 130, 141, 177, 180
huts, egg-collectors', 121-3, 126-8
Hyena, 117-18, 120

Ihu-arero, 84
Iko, excavation of rampart of, 187-8
Incas, 176; building techniques of, 178, 179, 180, 181; ceramics of, 127
Indonesia, 194, 196
Indus Valley, 157, 171
irrigation, 66, 97

Jablonowski (scholar), 196
Jaussen, Bishop Tepano, 13, 14, 90, 106, 109-15, 140, 142,

Jaussen, *cont.*,
143, 169, 172, 198
Juan Fernandez, 18, 50, 66, 148

Kerekorio, 82, 104, 209
Kerguelen (explorer), 49
kings, list of, 209
Klitin, Oleg, 169
Knorozov, Professor, 172
Knu-rau-ta-hui, 135
kohau rongo-rongo, 13, 113, 125,
140, 141, 155, 175, 190; *see
also* hieroglyphs *and rongo-
rongo*
Kon-Tiki, 175
Koreto, 106
Koster, Jobon, 18
Kotatake, Mount, 128, 130
Kotzebue, 62, 63
Kronstadt, 57, 109
Kruzensztern, Captain J.F., 57,
61
Kudriawcew, Boris, 169, 170

La Ferte-Mace, 102
La Pérouse, Count of, 49-56
Lavachery, Henri, 158, 159, 167,
176
Langara, Don Cayetano de, 36
Langle, Captain, 50, 52, 53, 54
language of the islanders, 42,
114, 196
Lazarus, 187, 189-90
legends, 74, 77, 83-8, 112, 194
Leningrad, 169, 170
Lima, 29, 90, 159
linguistic research, 196
linguistic skills, islanders', 35, 38
Lisjanski, Captain, 57, 58, 59,
60, 61
long-eared ones, 187;
descendants of, 182, 185,
187; and short-eared ones,
conflict between, 86-7, 188
Lorient, 157
Luka, 131

Madeira, 109, 147

Magellan Straits, 147
Mahatoua, 112
Mahine, 45-6
Mahuta Ariiki, king, 134, 209
Make-Make, 76, 77, 78, 80, 120,
123, 127, 133, 134
Mana, 145, 147-8, 152, 155
Mangareva, 91, 103, 110, 111,
147, 165, 192, 194, 195
Manila, 29
Manu, 73-81
Maoris, 193, 194, 201
maps of the island, 10, 35, 36, 50
Maraerenga, 83, 85, 86, 141
Marae-toe-hau, 194
Marion (explorer), 49
Marquesas, 90, 175, 192, 194,
196, 201
Mas-a-fuera, 63, 64, 67
Mataveri, 75, 78, 80, 84, 100,
101, 118, 120, 128, 142,
149, 151, 162, 163
Maurata, king, 82, 83, 88, 143,
209
Mea Kahi, 74
Mercator, 167
Merlet (entrepreneur), 107, 150
Metoro Taouaoure, 112-14, 198
Metraux, Dr, 158-61, 163, 165-7,
184, 187, 197
Meyer (scholar), 196
Miklucho-Maklaj, Nikolay, 109-
12, 169; his description of
tablets and hieroglyphs,
169-70
mission, founding of a, 89-105
moai, 11, 33, 66; *see also* statues,
stone
Moerenhout, J.A., 56, 193-4
Mohendzo-Daro, 157, 197
Mohican, 125, 140
Moko-Pingei, 87
Montinon, Father Albert, 89-91
Mordwinow, Admiral, 57
Morrison, Mr, 162
Motu Hao Hao, 73, 75
Motu Iti, 73, 75, 119, 123
Motu Kao, 123

Motu Nui, 73, 75, 78, 79, 80, 123, 190
Motu Torema Hiva, 77
Mulloy, Dr William, 178, 179, 181, 185, 204
Musée de l'Homme, 158

Nadiezda, 57, 58, 60
Nancy, 63, 64
New Caledonia, 149
New Guinea, 109, 111
New Hebrides, 196
New Mexico, 183
New Zealand, 158, 194, 196, 201
Newa, 57, 58, 59, 60, 61
Ngaara, king, 15, 209
North-West Passage, 65
Notre Dame de Paix, 103
Nukahiwa, 61

Ob, 172
O'Higgins, 110, 118, 140
Olderogge, Professor, 170, 172
Oliviera, Father Pacome, 89, 102
Oparo, 195
Oreo-Oreo, 122
origins of the Polynesian islanders, 15-16, 157-8, 179-80, 193-201; South American theory, 173, 175-6, 194, 195
Orito, 121, 134
Orongo, 75, 78, 80, 196; stone huts at, 121-3, 125, 126-8, 130
Ororoina, 182
Otaheite, 42

Paina, 96
Pakemio, 190
Pana, 92, 93, 94
Panama Canal, 147, 203
Papeete, 90, 91, 109, 111
Parry, Captain, 65
Patten, Dr, 42
Peard, Lieutenant, 67, 70
Penas Bay, 157

Peru, 29, 30, 31, 81, 90, 127, 141, 175, 176, 178
Peterson, Charles, 204
Philippi, Professor, 117
Philippines, 29
Pitcairn Island, 192, 201
platforms, stone (*ahu*), 11-12, 44, 55, 81, 86, 128-9, 133, 136-9, 155, 167, 176; excavation of, 178, 180, 181; names of, 137-9; restoration of, 204
Poike, 77, 187
Poiku, 86
Poro, Vincent, 149, 161
Potu-te-rangi, 87
Powaliszyn, Lieut. Paul, 60-1
presents given to islanders, 20, 32, 43, 51, 60, 163, 178
Prinz Eitel Friedrich, 153
Puakalika, 131

quarrying stone, 182-5

Rahi, 73-81
Raiatea, 201
Rangi-te-manu, 80
Rano Kao, 75, 86, 118, 120, 121, 125, 145
Rano Raraku, 11, 84, 118, 120, 131, 132, 134, 135, 139, 149, 173, 179, 182, 183, 185
Rapahango, Victoria, 162
Rarotongo, 195
religious beliefs, 24, 45, 53, 135
Resolution, 41, 42
Rigault-de-Genouilly, 157
Ritchie, Lieutenant, D.R., 145
Rivet, Paul, 158
Roggeveen, Arent, 18
Roggeveen, Admiral Jacob, 17-27, 178
Roma, 110, 104
rongo-rongo, 13-15, 105, 110-15, 117, 157, 169-73, 190, 197, 198, 204; see also *kohau rongo-rongo*

Rosendahl, Captain, 18-19
Roussel, Father Hippolite, 102-
    4, 106, 110, 111, 113
Royal Anthropological Institute,
    140
royal premises, excavation of,
    178
Rue, 75, 76, 78, 80
Rumancow, Duke, 57
Ruryk, 62
Russian expeditions, 57-64, 172-
    3
Russo-American Company, 57,
    61

Sacred Bird, ceremony of the ,
    75-80, 124
Sala-y-Gomez reef, 31n, 66, 77
Salmon, Mr, 106, 118, 119, 121,
    125, 126, 130, 140, 142
Samoa, 117, 194, 195, 196
San Lorenzo, 30-2
Santa Rosalia, 30-1
Santiago, 90, 110, 111, 117, 140,
    170
Scoresby-Routledge, Katherine,
    145, 147-56, 176, 184, 187
scurvy, 41-2
short-eared ones, *see* long-eared
    ones
skulls, typological analysis of,
    195
slavery, 81-2, 90, 106, 110, 177
sledges, 186-7
Smith, Dr Carlyle, 178, 180, 187
Smith, Mr, 162, 163-4
Smithsonian Institution, 143
societies, communal, 54
Society Islands, 194, 201
Solomon Islands, 196, 197
South Pole, 41
Southampton, 147
Spanish expedition, 29-39, 50
Spithead, 65
statues, stone, 11-13, 66, 158,
    181; design of, 135; Dutch
    description of, 24-5;

English impression of, 44-
    5; erection of, 133, 181-2,
    185-6, 204; French
    description of, 53, 55;
    making of, 132, 182-5;
    moving of, 132, 181, 186-7;
    number of, 182; of red
    stone, 179; overthrown, 12,
    44-5, 181; restoration of,
    203-4; seen by Americans,
    129, 130, 132-6; seen by
    Germans, 119; seen by
    Russians, 58-9, 61, 62;
    Spanish description of, 32-
    3
Suerte, 91

tablets, wooden, *see rongo-rongo*
Tafai, 195
Tahiti, 90-1, 105, 106, 109, 110,
    111, 118, 140, 143, 147,
    194, 196, 201
Tamateka, 101
Tampico, 105
tangata rongo-rongo, 14, 15
tau, 200, 204
Tau-ko-ihu, 85
Te Ira-ka-tea, 83
Te-pito-te-henua, 73, 77, 83, 84
Te Rangi Hiroa, 194
Tehaki, 112
Temanu, 95
Teoni, 99
Tepano, Juan, 165-7
Tepito, 82, 83, 209
Teraai mountain, 136
Terano, 119
Teresa Ramos, 102
Terra Australis Nondum
    Incognita, 17, 18, 29, 41,
    49
Terra de Davis, sighting of, 17-
    18
Terra Incognita, *see* Terra
    Australis Nondum
    Incognita
Thienhoven, 17-23